high-vibrational *thinking*

how to

T0353173

beat
the
blues

anxiety, worry,
depression
and troubles

high-vibrational *thinking* HVT

how to
beat
the
blues

anxiety, worry,
depression
and troubles

steve wharton

foulsham
LONDON • NEW YORK • TORONTO • SYDNEY

foulsham

The Publishing House, Bennetts Close, Cippenham,
Slough, Berkshire, SL1 5AP, England

Foulsham books can be found in all good bookshops and
direct from www.foulsham.com

ISBN 13: 978-0-572-03177-0
ISBN 10: 0-572-03177-7

Copyright © 2006 Steve Wharton

Cover photograph © Superstock

A CIP record for this book is available from the British Library

Printed in Great Britain by Cox & Wyman Ltd, Reading, Berkshire

Contents

What Is Depression?

The *Collins Dictionary* describes depression as a 'mental state in which a person has feelings of gloom and inadequacy'. The *Cassell Concise Dictionary* describes depression as 'a mental disorder characterised by low spirits, reduction of self-esteem and lowering of energy'.

Depression is an illness that makes you feel down and dejected over a long period of time. You may feel sad and empty inside, accompanied by a sense of hopelessness. You may have great difficulty just coping with everyday things and any form of responsibility can feel like an almost unbearable burden. Functioning on a day-to-day basis becomes increasingly difficult and you feel like you want to withdraw from society. It has a negative effect on most areas of your life; your relationships, work, social life and personal hygiene can all suffer.

Depression can affect anyone at any age and causes a disruption of brain chemicals creating an imbalance. It is usually triggered by stressful or traumatic events that we all encounter at certain points in our lives. Money, relationships and work are the general areas that these events originate from.

How this book works

The first section of this book explains what high-vibrational thinking is and how it works.

The second section shows you how to use high-vibrational thinking to gain a greater understanding of depression and why you may be experiencing it in your life. Using high-vibrational thinking – or HVT – will enable you to identify the reasons why you may suffer from depression and give you the tools to do something about it. This new and empowering way of looking at this problem can help put you back in control and enable practical positive steps to be taken in order to release you from this illness. HVT breaks it down to the basics and this is what is so important, as dealing with it becomes much easier once you clearly see it for what it is.

This new, fresh approach, coupled with some simple basics of psychology, makes this book easy and uncomplicated to read, making it accessible to people from all walks of life, who are just looking for some simple answers to a problem that can affect anyone.

Our World of Energy

'If you want to find the secrets of the universe, think in terms of energy, frequency and vibration.' Dr Nikola Tesla, 1942

Dr Nikola Tesla was one of the foremost scientists of the early 20th Century. His outstanding intellect paved the way for a large number of modern technological developments; in fact, the tesla coil is still used in many television sets today. It is amazing to think that his words in 1942 should still be so relevant today. We now know that his understanding of the universe as energy, frequency and vibration was quite accurate. As we explore the intricate workings of the universe, unlocking the secrets of this amazing world of energy in which we live, this fact only becomes clearer.

Nothing you see around you is quite as it seems! The world that we live in is a huge ocean of energy, taking many different forms. The age of the microscope has shown us with abundant clarity that things that appear solid and static to us are in fact nothing of the sort. Even if the only science you know has been learnt from TV dramas about forensic scientists, you will be aware that if you look at an apparently solid object at a sufficiently powerful magnification, you will find that it is made up not from a single solid substance but from tiny particles vibrating at phenomenal speed. These tiny particles are known as neutrons, electrons and protons, and they link together to form atoms, the most basic building blocks of life.

What is perhaps even more astonishing is that atoms actually consist of 90 per cent empty space, which – by logical deduction – means that what we think of as solid, such as a concrete wall, is in fact mostly not solid at all! Nothing around us is actually solid, even though it may appear so; everything is made up of energy, vibrating constantly and at high frequency. This applies to everything you see around you: trees, houses, cars, walls, roads, dogs, cats, fish. It is a fundamental law of physics and applies even to us humans.

Each of these millions upon millions of different forms of energy vibrates at a specific frequency. The frequency at which it vibrates influences the form of the object. For example, the molecules of a solid vibrate very slowly; the molecules of a liquid vibrate more quickly; and the molecules of a gas vibrate even more quickly. Thus something with the same chemical composition can take different forms, depending on the vibrational frequency of its molecules. When the molecules are vibrating at their usual frequency rate, water appears as a liquid. Slow down that frequency and you get ice; speed up the frequency and you get steam.

We are all part of the energy exchange
As I have said, we are just as much a part of this cycle of energy as everything else around us. High-vibrational thinking (HVT) is based on that fact. Its fundamental principle is that we need to learn to see and think about our world in terms of energy.

High-vibrational thinking is a revolutionary new concept that taps into our knowledge of the movement of energy throughout the universe. It offers a way of seeing people – and the interactions between people – as part of a unique energy-transmission process that is hugely empowering to the individual. The first part of this book explains exactly how the system works. If you go back to fundamentals, it is really very easy to understand.

Just as ice, water and steam vibrate at different frequencies, so emotional energy also vibrates at different frequencies. As I will be explaining in detail later, positive emotions are high-vibrational energies, while negative emotions are low-vibrational energies. If we can find a way to maintain high-vibrational energy and deflect low-vibrational energy, then we can change our whole perspective on life. That's what HVT can help us to do. HVT is a system that takes positive thinking on to a whole new level.

HVT changes your perspective

This realisation throws a whole new light on how we perceive our world. Indeed, knowing how to use this information – and I'll be showing you that, too – can be hugely liberating and empowering, because it offers a way of using our knowledge to handle our lives in a more beneficial and productive way. This new perspective gives you far greater control over everyday situations and events you may previously have thought were largely beyond your control. With this knowledge comes power, and that power is the ability to choose more carefully how you relate to the energies that affect your life.

HVT will become automatic

What's more, once you have learned how to use this power, it will become an automatic way of thinking, and you can gain the benefits without even having to make a conscious choice about it. Once you have learnt to walk, you don't need to think about the process consciously any more. It's the same with HVT. Once you understand HVT, you will find that you automatically begin to incorporate it into your life as a working practice without any conscious effort on your part. Its positive influence on your life will be automatic, as the truth of HVT, once learned, cannot be ignored. Using HVT on a daily basis becomes a natural habit that will benefit every aspect of your life and help you to change in a positive and fulfilling way. All of a sudden, you will find that something inside you is monitoring the events and situations in your life and automatically responding to a negative situation in a way that will prevent it from dragging down the frequency of your energy field and making you feel bad.

A paradigm shift in consciousness occurs, and you find yourself able to deal with the negative events and situations that are part of everyday life in a new and positive way. HVT enables you to take control of events and situations rather than allowing them to control you. This is incredibly liberating, freeing your mind to direct your life in a much more productive and focused way.

Let's look at a simple example from one HVT course I have recently run. Within days of attending a course, two of my students found themselves turning off a particular television programme that they had been watching regularly for many years. They did not think about this action consciously until weeks later when it came up in conversation. Another student was talking about how negative this television programme had become. At that point, they both realised they had made the decision not to watch it any more immediately after attending the HVT course. Subconsciously, they had sensed its negative impact and put a stop to it.

This kind of reaction is common among people who attend HVT courses, because they quickly learn to avoid engaging with damaging negative energies. You are already starting to learn that lesson simply by reading this book.

You too can learn automatically to handle situations and decisions in a more positive and beneficial way.

Essentially simple

The real strength of HVT is its simplicity and the fact that when applied to any subject it breaks down to a few basics. This enables anybody, whatever their age or background, to gain an understanding that previously may have seemed impossible. This is one of the reasons we have had so much success in working with children as young as 10 years old. Young people absorb the concept very quickly and find it easy to think in terms of HVT about every area of their life.

It also means that the technique can be applied to any aspect of your life, regardless of your occupation or lifestyle. At school, it can give you more confidence and enthusiasm and help you to perform well. At work, it can cut negativity, create a better atmosphere and even increase productivity. In the home, it can reduce arguments and create a more loving environment.

Essentially, HVT is about making you feel good about yourself and maintaining that feel-good factor whatever life throws at you. Just think how much happier that could make you – not to mention the immeasurable stride forward in terms of moving our world into a brighter, high-vibrational future.

How Emotional Energy Vibrates

Now we understand that the whole world is part of a complex energy system, let's look specifically at how that affects us. Here, we are talking in terms of the power of emotional energy, and that is what we can harness to work to our advantage with HVT.

We have seen that – just like the objects around us – we are made up of energy and – like all forms of energy – our personal energy field vibrates constantly. The vibrational frequency of our energy field is affected by our thoughts and feelings. These are also made up of energy waves and influence our lives much more than we may realise. So depending on how we are feeling at any given time, the frequency at which our energy field vibrates can change dramatically.

Scientists and researchers in the USA have measured the frequency of the energy waves transmitted by the emotion of love, which they found vibrate very quickly, or at a very high frequency. Similarly, they measured the frequency of the energy waves transmitted by the emotion of fear, which they found vibrate very slowly, or at a low frequency. Our world exists within these two parameters.

*Love is transmitted on a short wavelength, so it has a fast,
high-vibrational frequency.*

*Fear is transmitted on a long wavelength, so it has a slow,
low-vibrational frequency.*

Think for a moment about listening to the radio, and this
will help you to understand how it works. Radio stations
are constantly transmitting radio waves. These are in the
air all around us, even though we cannot actually see
them. If your radio is not tuned into the right frequency,
all you will hear is an annoying hiss. However, if you tune
in your radio to the right frequency, you will be able to
pick up on those radio waves so that you can hear and
understand them perfectly, whether they are transmitting
music, news, drama or comedy.

Happy is a high vibration
So whatever we are thinking and feeling has a very real
effect, as it alters the frequency of our personal energy
field. If we are happy, our energy is high-vibrational; if we
are sad, our energy is low-vibrational. I am sure you are
already getting the idea. Similarly, we can be affected by
other people's thoughts and feelings. If you are unlucky
enough to be in a room full of bored or unhappy people, it
is very hard to remain upbeat and cheerful.

When we are full of laughter and joy, it makes us feel good. What is actually happening is that the high-vibrational energy of joy has pushed up the frequency of our personal energy field. We experience the same effect when we achieve something good, such as passing a driving test or an exam, scoring a goal, winning a competition or receiving praise for a job well done. What is happening here is the same: the achievement has suddenly made us feel successful and good about ourselves, again pushing up the frequency of our personal energy field.

So, as you can see, any thoughts and feelings that are positive – laughter, joy, honesty, sincerity, truth, compassion – are high-vibrational, keeping our energy field vibrating at the higher levels and therefore making us feel good. Just think about some of the expressions we use to describe that kind of feeling: 'I'm high as a kite', 'I'm buzzing', 'My mind's racing'. They clearly demonstrate that great feeling we get when we feel good, and they are referring to the frequency of our personal energy field. The faster our energy field vibrates, the better we feel, because that means we are closer to the frequency of love.

Of course, the opposite is also true. Anger, frustration, hate, jealousy, envy, greed and selfishness are all negative thoughts and feelings. Such emotions are low-vibrational; they slow down our energy field and make us feel bad. This is why we use phrases such as 'I'm down in the dumps' or 'I'm flat as a pancake'. The lower our energy field vibrates, the closer we are to the vibration of fear – which is not where we want to be!

Increasing our vibrational frequency

Even though this may be the first time you have thought about it in these terms, you probably will recognise that we spend most of our time trying to feel good about ourselves. In HVT terms, that means we are constantly seeking to increase our vibrational energy frequency.

There are any number of ways to try to do this – getting your hair done, buying a new car, having a drink, going out with friends, buying new clothes. They can all be effective, but if they don't affect your fundamental emotional state, the effect is not going to last very long. If you have ever got a buzz from buying a new pair of shoes, only to feel low again by the time you got home because you had nowhere to go to show them off, you'll know what I mean.

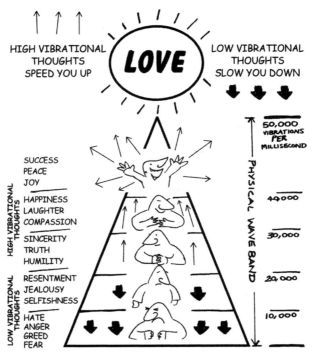

Hypothetically speaking, the physical waveband may run from 0 to 50,000 vibrations per millisecond. Our energy fields fluctuate between these parameters in our day-to-day lives. When we are happy and enjoying life, we may be vibrating at 35,000 vibrations per millisecond, but this may fall to 6,000 vibrations per millisecond when we are down in the dumps.

Some people take the search for a high to extremes, possibly drinking too much and experimenting with drugs. This may give a temporary 'high' but can very soon have the serious negative result of addiction.

That's where HVT comes in, because it is a way of educating ourselves so that our normal vibrational frequency is higher – plus it teaches us to control the effect of low-vibrational energy from other sources. It's just like exercising regularly to increase your resting heart rate. This not only makes you feel fitter, but it also makes it easier for you to cope with the physical demands of your everyday life.

How Our Emotional Frequency Is Established

As we spend most of our time trying to raise our vibrational frequency in order to feel better about ourselves, it makes sense to have a look at the factors that determine our individual energy level in the first place. This energy level is established and controlled primarily by our subconscious mind.

The conscious and subconscious mind

Your conscious mind is what you use to go about your everyday life – paying the bills, cleaning, sorting the washing, going to work. This is the methodical, reasoning part of your mind that carries out the daily tasks. It is the organised, sensible, logical part of you that understands how your world works. Your conscious mind automatically analyses any situation it confronts and plots the best and most logical way to deal with it.

Your subconscious mind, on the other hand, is a more complex entity, and is a source of immense power. It is affected by your surroundings in much more subtle ways and reacts most strongly to emotional stimuli.

Many psychologists refer to the subconscious mind as the 'inner child', because they feel that this best describes its characteristics. This terminology can help us to understand why our subconscious can sometimes pull us towards something that is not good for us. Imagine yourself as a child of five years old, with all the feelings and wonderment you had at that age; now imagine that this child is real and living inside you. Now you have a picture of your subconscious mind. It does not reflect you as you are now, with everything you have experienced and learnt over the course of a lifetime, but you as you were then. This child has no concept of what is good or bad for

Your inner child (your subconscious mind) will do everything it can to keep you in your comfort zone, even if this means holding you back in your life.

you; it just has its programming, which it will try to stick to regardless of what you may or may not consciously want.

In other words, we are all going through life trying to make some kind of progress but subject to the limitations that our subconscious mind places upon us. In terms of energy, our subconscious monitors us on a daily basis to keep us in what it has defined as our normal vibrational frequency zone.

Our formative years

The most important factor in determining this normal or average vibrational frequency level is the first five or six years of our lives. It is during these formative years that we establish our general thought patterns about ourselves. These early years effectively programme our subconscious mind with certain beliefs about ourselves and how we see the world around us, which we then carry throughout the rest of our lives and which are very difficult to change. This vibrational frequency programming sets the boundaries for us and has a major bearing on every aspect of our life from then on.

The most influential factors in our development are our immediate family and the environment we grow up in. In other words, the vibrational frequency of our environment and the frequency level of our family are what we pick up and become used to as our norm. When our mind is young and impressionable during those early years, we readily accept the situation in which we find ourselves. Because we don't know of any other situation, we unquestioningly believe that this is where we belong. This becomes the frequency zone we feel comfortable in and which, subconsciously, we spend virtually the rest of our lives trying to stay in.

So if you were brought up in a family with not much love (high-vibrational energy), you will believe that you don't deserve much love, and your subconscious will use all its power to make sure that that is what happens. This will have massive repercussions, affecting your relationships, your work – in fact, everything you do in life. Your subconscious will stick to the programming, whether it's good for you or bad for you. In other words, it will monitor your vibrational frequency and keep it at the level that it is programmed to do.

As we grow up, our subconscious beliefs tend to become self-confirming because we constantly play them over in our subconscious mind, reaffirming our opinions and thoughts about ourselves. Most of the time, we are completely unaware that we are doing this. When we are constantly affirming to ourselves that we are not worthy (worthy meaning deserving of love, the highest-vibrational energy), we are keeping our vibrational frequency at the lower levels – and making life much harder for ourselves. The opposite is also true. If we constantly circulate high-vibrational thoughts about ourselves, we will keep our vibrational frequency at the higher levels, which in turn affirms that we are worthy and makes our life run much more smoothly.

Your inner child (subconscious mind) is much more in control of your life than you realise.

Of course, we have to acknowledge that we are all different and unique individuals with many varying factors determining our personality. This is why different people emerge from a similar upbringing with a different attitude to life. However, you are almost certainly reading this book because at least one aspect of your life can be improved, and understanding where any negative input may have come from is the first step towards being able to change the negative and maximise the positive.

The comfort zone

The energy level that we feel is where we belong is often referred to as our 'comfort zone'. We find it very difficult to break out of this zone, as our subconscious mind constantly draws us back to it as its starting point, regardless of whether it is in fact good for us or bad for us. This may seem strange, but in fact is quite logical.

We tend to mix and feel more comfortable with people of a similar vibration rate.

You may, for example, feel uncomfortable in an upmarket, expensive restaurant, or perhaps you feel nervous when talking to professional people, such as lawyers or consultants. What you are experiencing is a reaction to the frequency of the environment or person. If the frequency is vibrating at a higher rate than yours, you will probably feel slightly uncomfortable. This means you will seek out places and people with which you share a similar frequency, as this is where you naturally feel most comfortable.

Imagine carrying around with you an identity card that has not only all your personal details but also all your unconscious beliefs about yourself printed on it. If your normal vibrational frequency is low, your ID might list some of the following:

▶ You will only be shown a limited amount of affection from people who are close to you
▶ You are only allowed to have a low-paid job
▶ You are only allowed to live in a small house
▶ You are only allowed to have an old car
▶ You are only allowed to be average in what you do
▶ You are only allowed to wear casual clothes
▶ You are only allowed to achieve a limited amount of success
▶ You are only allowed to have difficult relationships
▶ You are only allowed to have friends who take advantage of you

Now imagine that if you try to step out of line by going against these guidelines, you will be confronted by a police officer whose job it is to keep you within their confines. Let's say you manage to get a good job that pays well. Before you know it, the officer is on your case and starts talking you out of the job. You may find that you can't motivate yourself to raise your level of achievement as you need to in order to do the job well, so you start to make excuses and lay the blame elsewhere. Instead, you tell yourself that you work too hard or the firm is taking advantage of you, the pay is not adequate or you are not appreciated. This undermines your confidence and your ability to do the job well, and before very long you will find a way to give up the job while blaming everyone else.

I have seen this happen in my own experience. A very capable employee suddenly, after about three months in the job, begins to under perform. They start coming in late with any feeble excuse, they cultivate an attitude of not being appreciated, they disrupt the other staff and in the end they push you so far that you have no choice but to let them go. When this happens, they insist that they are being victimised, they have done nothing wrong, and they may even threaten to take you to a tribunal. What they fail to acknowledge – even to themselves – is that it is their own behaviour that has caused the problem. The police officer has done his job and dragged them back into their low-vibrational comfort zone.

The problem with this situation is that we don't realise what is happening – that it is our own subconscious mind that is wreaking such havoc in our lives. It does not seem logical to believe that we would sabotage our own efforts, so we assume that the fault lies elsewhere.

I have experienced this myself, so I know how easily it can occur. When I was at school I was quite good at sport and soon found myself playing for the school teams. I did very well, and at one point it was expected that I might go on to a higher level. Once I realised that this was in prospect, I couldn't seem to motivate myself any more and decided to stop playing altogether. At the time, I just decided that I didn't feel like playing any more; it was only years later that I realised what had taken place. The threat of success had triggered off my subconscious programming, which dictated that I didn't deserve the high-frequency feelings that success could bring. These would have pushed me out of my comfort zone and into a new higher-frequency zone, so my subconscious mind convinced me that I didn't like sports any more and made me feel tired and unmotivated when faced with a game. Unfortunately for me, my subconscious won, and at 14 years old I hung up my boots and missed many years of enjoyment.

Not better but different

One thing always to remember, however, is that even if you start out with a low-vibrational energy field and feel uncomfortable with a different group of people, they are not 'better' than you. We all have our own qualities, strengths and weaknesses. You may want to be more like someone who has a high-vibrational energy field because they are fun to be around and are positive and more successful – that's fine. But that doesn't make them intrinsically better than you. Envy and self-criticism are both low-vibrational emotions, and if you give way to them, it will only make things worse.

You may, on the other hand, be someone who has had a good upbringing in a high-vibrational environment, leaving you with high-vibrational thought patterns. This gives you a much better chance of making the most of your life and better equips you to take advantage of opportunities that arise. You may still feel uncomfortable in places or with people where the energy pattern does not match your own – probably because your personal energy field is vibrating at a higher frequency. But it is important that you do not fall into the trap of believing that this makes you better in some way, for this is a damaging thought pattern. Arrogance and self-importance will pull down your energy frequency.

Don't try to place blame

It is important to point out here that your parents and their parents before them were also subject to this subconscious programming. However they brought you up, they were doing their best within their own programmed mental confines.

It is essential that you do not try to attach blame to anybody for your life as it stands at the moment. This would be to go straight down the low-vibrational route. Such thought processes are negative and low-frequency; they are certain to act as a dead weight around your neck and pull you down. Pointing the finger at others serves no purpose and will only harm you – by lowering your vibrational frequency. This is the time to assess the past and move on to the new, high-vibrational you.

How Our Emotional Frequency Affects Our Lives

The easiest way to demonstrate how limiting it can be to allow your subconscious mind to remain in control of your life is to take a look at a few examples.

Paul's comfort zone with crime

A few years ago, my work brought me into contact with a sales representative who proceeded to tell me a bit about himself. Let's call him Paul. Paul was brought up in a fairly tough environment, and his father had not been around much, as he had spent most of his time in prison for relatively minor offences. However, this childhood grounding had taken its toll, and at 12 years old Paul had found himself in trouble with the police for the first time, for a minor crime. His family considered crime as a profession and accepted it as a normal way of life so, far from chastising him for having committed a crime, they were more concerned that he had not got away with it. This pathway continued. Paul's teenage years were littered with offences, but since he was behaving exactly according to his own idea of normality, he could see nothing unacceptable in this.

At the age of 25, during another stay in prison, Paul decided to go straight. He left prison with good intentions, found himself a job and at first managed to stay on the straight and narrow. But it wasn't long before he found himself drawn back to crime, however hard he tried not to be tempted. When I spoke to him, he was very disappointed with himself and said that no matter how hard he tried, he kept committing offences. Even though this made him feel bad about himself, when the temptation was there, he just could not resist it.

I wish I could tell you that this story has a happy ending, but I lost contact with Paul many years ago and do not know how his life has turned out. However, over the years I have given Paul's story a great deal of thought. When I began to understand the workings of the subconscious mind, it became clear to me exactly what his problem was. Even though Paul wanted to stop being drawn to crime, his subconscious mind (inner child) did not. To his subconscious mind, crime was defined as normal behaviour – because this is what it had been programmed with during his first five or six years – and so was safely in his comfort zone. When, as an adult, Paul wanted to break out of his comfort zone, his subconscious mind took every opportunity to draw him back in.

When you think about how deep-rooted and fundamental our subconscious mind is to our entire personality, it is hardly surprising that it is very influential. We all have to contend with the daily tussle with our subconscious mind, but when we understand that it is simply trying to keep us within the boundaries of our own comfort zone, we have taken the first step towards doing something to take control over it.

Sue's comfort zone with food

Another friend of mine – let's call her Sue – has spent the last year or so trying to lose weight, something many of us have struggled with at some time. She has tried every kind of diet, with the same results: she loses a few pounds at the beginning, but a few weeks later the weight is back on. Then it's on to the next diet regime. She has fallen into the trap of yo-yo dieting and is unable to maintain her ideal weight for any length of time. So why is it so difficult for Sue – like many of us – to get into new eating habits and stick to them?

Let's take a careful look at what is happening here. When Sue begins the diet, she really wants to lose weight and is fully motivated. She has the necessary willpower to control her eating habits. She knows that she will feel better and be healthier if she eats well and maintains the right weight for her height and build. The principles are easy enough to understand: eat the right amount of the right foods and she will lose weight; and with the range of healthy food options available, there is not even any need for her to feel hungry. Nevertheless, after the first few weeks, or even days, she finds herself drifting back into bad eating habits. Sue's favourite tactic is to move the goal posts. Having decided that she wanted to lose weight for an up-and-coming holiday, she then decides it's for her daughter's graduation ceremony, then for Christmas, and so on.

The problem is, of course, that Sue is obeying her inner child. Her subconscious is telling her that the unhealthy diet she has drifted into is what she should be eating. This kind of food is her comfort zone and it is very difficult to leave it. 'No, you can't have any chocolate or sweets and you must eat plenty of fresh vegetables' isn't what Sue's inner child wants to hear. Sue's initial determination will control the child for a while, but very soon the child's persistence will be rewarded because it just feels right to go back to your comfort zone.

Jim's comfort zone with keeping fit

Jim's story is another example of how the subconscious mind sabotages our efforts to instigate change. When Jim first went to the gym he was filled with enthusiasm and energy for his get-fit project. Sure enough, the first few visits were easy, as he raced around the equipment, lifting weights, doing sit-ups and so on, quite possibly overdoing it in his eagerness to succeed. Then, after a while, the novelty wore off. Jim started to accept the feeblest excuses for not going to the gym – 'I have to take the dog for a walk', 'I feel a bit tired' and (an old favourite of many of us) 'I haven't got time'. Of course, just as Jim's initial determination had begun to wear off, his subconscious mind had kicked in, renewing its bid to regain control and pull Jim back into his lazy comfort zone.

Your subconscious mind acts just like a child and soon gets bored.

Just imagine taking a five-year-old child to the gym with you. At first they may be excited and full of energy, dragging you around the gym and trying out all the equipment. This might continue for two or three visits, but then the child would begin to get bored and start whingeing about having to go. You would end up virtually dragging them there, and while you doggedly followed your keep-fit programme, the child would probably be sitting in the corner sulking.

This is exactly what happens in reality, only it's your inner child that behaves in this way. You don't realise that this is what is going on; you just feel the symptoms. Your enthusiasm drops, you feel tired, you look for excuses not to go, and the next thing you know, you haven't been for weeks and you regret taking out a gym membership that commits you to the next – very expensive – six months.

Familiar story? I know it's happened to me on more than one occasion. Yet again, it's the subconscious mind dragging us back into our comfort zone. No wonder it is so hard to go forward in life when the most restricting factor is hidden in our own head. But remember: knowing what's going on is the first step towards being able to do something about it.

Jeff and Dave's stories

Another way to explore the notion of the comfort zone is to compare two people with similar upbringings. Jeff and Dave had known each other all their lives. They grew up together on a housing estate in a typical working-class environment. Their birthdays were only three days apart, and as children they were inseparable.

Jeff was the youngest of five children, with two brothers and two sisters. Life was quite hard for them, as their father and mother had separated when Jeff was only five years old, and during the time before the separation the house had been filled with arguments and anger as his parents struggled to cope. Jeff's father had never held down a job for long and spent most of his time drinking and gambling away the family's money on the horses. Money was therefore scarce, and Jeff had to rely on hand-me-down clothes from his older brothers. The family always had enough to eat, but there was no money for life's luxuries, such as holidays, treats or days out. All these factors combined to mean that the primary emotions surrounding Jeff in his formative years were anger, worry, self-pity, hostility, fear and a general sense of having less than everybody else.

As you will now recognise, all these emotions are low-vibrational. Naturally, they contributed hugely to how Jeff felt about himself. He felt that he wasn't as good as most of the other children because they seemed to have lots more than him, so his habitual thought patterns about himself were low-frequency: 'I don't deserve', 'I'm not as good as other people' and 'I can't do anything' were the kind of statements he would unconsciously repeat to himself. This negativity became Jeff's norm. His subconscious mind believed this was what he deserved to be, and it set about ensuring that this was what he got for the rest of his life.

Jeff was a very good soccer player and made the school team, but he found it hard to motivate himself and missed many chances of furthering his progress. He was quite bright but somehow could never be bothered to try hard enough, so he failed most of his exams. He could have made the swimming team but found an excuse so that he didn't have to take part.

When he left school, Jeff found work with an insurance company as a sales representative. He did okay, but somehow he was never going to be one of the high flyers. After a few years in this job he decided that selling insurance was too much like hard work and that he would do much better in a new job, even though some of the other reps were making good money and doing very well. He always had his own reasons for why they did better than him. It was because they had better areas than him or easier policies to sell. One thing was for sure: it was never his fault. So Jeff continued moving from one job to the next over the next few years, not really getting on in any of them, because – according to Jeff – the other reps always had it better in some way. In the end, he put it down to the fact that he just didn't have any luck.

The crucial fact that Jeff wasn't aware of was that he himself was in control of his seeming lack of good fortune. His subconscious mind – programmed to believe that Jeff

Dave and Jeff had totally different outlooks on life: Dave was positive, Jeff was negative.

deserved to stay at a low frequency level – was monitoring his life all the way along. In order to keep him at his frequency level, it 'allowed' him only a very small amount of success – any more would have pushed him into a higher frequency zone. As soon as it looked as if he might become more successful, his subconscious mind kicked in and sabotaged any possibility of that happening. A little voice in Jeff's head would convince him that somebody had it in for him or he never got a fair chance or he should find another job because nobody in his current company appreciated him. This is how our subconscious mind keeps us within the comfort zone that it is programmed for.

Now let's take a look at Dave.

Dave was an only child whose parents doted on him. His father was a foreman at the local steel works and his mother a very loving woman who spent her time looking after the family and their home. Dave's home was filled with love and positive energy. He remembers that his parents very rarely argued or had any kind of disagreement. Dave grew up a very happy child, whose parents gave him lots of attention and constantly told him that they loved him. Being an only child, he wanted for nothing. He always had fashionable clothes and there were holidays abroad every year.

Growing up in this pleasant, loving, high-vibrational environment programmed Dave's subconscious mind to believe that this was the frequency zone in which he belonged. His habitual thought patterns about himself were positive: 'I know I can do it', 'I deserve the best', 'I am as good as anybody'.

Dave was never quite as good at soccer as Jeff, but he worked hard and with conviction, so he progressed further and made it to junior colts level with the local professional soccer club. Dave was not quite as bright as Jeff, but, again, he worked hard and eventually left school with good qualifications. After school, Dave followed Jeff into the insurance business and also became a sales representative. He always came in among the top two or three sales reps in the area. He loved his job, and his attitude impressed the management. He was soon promoted to area sales manager, then a few years later to regional sales director. Dave's life seemed charmed compared to Jeff's; everything always seemed to work out for him.

Jeff and Dave's friendship suffered over the years as their different life paths moved them into different social circles. Of course, they still spoke when they met, but after a while they found they had little in common, and their meetings became more of a passing hello than an in-depth conversation. In fact, Dave's success engendered not a little resentment in Jeff, which, sadly, estranged the two men even further.

Why our vibrational frequency is so important

Looking at Dave and Jeff's lives gives us an idea of how incredibly important our early years are in determining how easy the rest of our life is likely to be. Even though Dave was less talented and not as bright as Jeff, it was still much easier for him to be successful in life than it was for Jeff.

Dave's subconscious programming was of a much higher frequency than Jeff's. His feelings about himself and his own expectations were on a more high-vibrational frequency. He felt better about his abilities, so he had the confidence to try harder; he expected the best, so he impressed others with his positive attitude. All this enabled him to be successful at most of the things that he attempted. His subconscious mind monitored his life and kept him in the higher-frequency zone where it was programmed to believe he should be.

This meant that Dave saw life in a very different way from Jeff. What appeared to be insurmountable obstacles to

Dave had a much more high-frequency upbringing than Jeff, and this was the real difference between them.

Jeff were mere molehills to Dave. In a situation where Jeff's subconscious mind might say, 'That's just my luck; it will never work out for me', Dave's would say 'I'm always lucky; I know this will work for me'. Where Jeff's subconscious might say 'This job is a waste of time; everybody has an insurance policy', Dave's might say, 'I love this job; everybody needs insurance'. At higher frequency levels, life looks and feels completely different than it does at the lower levels. Jeff and Dave had exactly the same job, dealing with the same customers, and they had the same potential for success; the only difference was their vibrational frequency.

By now you will have a very clear idea of how our personal vibrational frequency can control our lives. You will soon begin to learn how HVT can help to change that frequency and put us back in control.

Frequency Variations

Before we move on to looking at how to start raising your vibrational frequency, there is one more issue to consider. That is how our average vibrational frequency changes naturally. Although it is true that the foundations of our subconscious, and therefore our average frequency level, are established at an early stage, our frequency level can and does change in relation to time, the people we interact with and the various challenges life presents us with.

We regularly encounter both high-vibrational and low-vibrational energy from inside and outside. First we are going to look at the energy we encounter from outside. How we cope with this on the inside is, of course, vital, so we'll look at this issue at the end of the chapter.

Frequency interaction

How we interact with other people has a major impact on our energy levels on a daily basis. In the case of Jeff and Dave (see page 35), we saw that Dave had a fundamentally positive, high-frequency energy, and because of this he made other people feel better too. The management recognised his potential, the customers were more responsive. This is because any interaction with another human being affects your frequency level. If you interact with somebody of a higher frequency, you will have your frequency pulled up; likewise, if you interact with a person of a lower frequency, you will be dragged down. This is why some people feel very draining to be with, whereas others feel uplifting.

A positive, high-frequency attitude is great to be around.

It's easy to demonstrate this effect just by thinking about a few of the people you know. If you are having a conversation with someone who is enthusiastic, there's lots of high-vibrational energy around. You can chat for hours without the conversation lagging. On the other hand, if you are having a conversation with someone who is unhappy, there's so much low-vibrational energy that you may struggle to keep the conversation going. You are being affected by this person's low-vibrational energies, as they are likewise affected by your vibrational frequency.

Let's pursue this a bit further. If you are yourself feeling down while you are trying to cheer someone else up, it will be much harder work. In fact, it's quite likely that you will both ending up crying into your beer! On the other hand, if you are feeling pretty good at the start of the conversation, the person that you are trying to cheer up might pull you down a bit, but it is more likely that you will be able to raise their spirits and help them to feel better.

The more you can be around high-vibrational energy, the more it will benefit your own energy levels on a daily basis; and if you are constantly around high-vibrational people, then the impact can help to stimulate a long-term improvement in your own energies. You really are fundamentally affected by the company you keep.

Places also have a vibrational frequency to which we react. We all have places that we love and others that we find intimidating or uncomfortable. Some towns feel depressing and unwelcoming, whereas other towns feel upbeat and pleasant. Here, we are simply picking up on the collective vibrational frequency of the people who live there.

Changing energy frequency levels

As we progress through our lives, we may find that we achieve success in different things – perhaps our career takes off and we become very good at what we do. This increases and reinforces our good opinion of ourselves, giving us more confidence in our own ability and changing our personal thought patterns. This means that our personal energy frequency rises. A similar negative effect can occur if you have a run of bad luck. If you find the problems you encounter too much to cope with, they are likely to depress your vibrational level.

We all experience natural vibrational fluctuations on a daily basis as we encounter and have to cope with life's everyday events. We have probably all experienced the feeling of being down in the dumps, when our problems seem huge and we can't see a way around them. If we have an interrupted night's sleep and wake up on a rainy day to news of a traffic jam on our route to work on local radio, it can make things feel even worse. But with a good night's sleep and a ray of sunshine when you open the curtains, you feel a new surge of energy and yesterday's problems diminish. What is happening is we are viewing the same situation from a different frequency level.

Anna's typical day

Let's imagine that during any given day we have 100,000 thoughts going through our mind. These thoughts are influenced by day-to-day activities – people we meet, situations we encounter, whether our favourite team wins or loses, news in the newspapers and so on. The thoughts we have may be high-vibrational or low-vibrational, and each one has an influence on the vibration rate of our personal energy field, speeding it up or slowing it down as we go about our daily activities. Let us take a look at a typical day to give you an idea of how it works.

8.00 a.m.

It's a bright spring morning, the sun is shining, and as Anna throws back the curtains, the sun's rays cascade into the bedroom, illuminating everything in a golden glow. This is one of those days when she feels on top of the world. The children are relaxed and happy as they get ready for school. Anna's thoughts are **high-vibrational**, she feels content. Her mind is untouched by any of the **low-vibrational** situations that we all encounter every day. At this point of the day, it's fair to assume that her personal energy field is vibrating at a fairly fast rate.

8.30 a.m.

This is a great start, but – hang on – little Lucy is lagging behind and holding everybody up. 'Come on, Lucy. Hurry up or you will be late for school,' shouts Anna. A slight feeling of frustration sweeps over her. This is a **low-vibrational** emotion, and it slows down Anna's personal energy field slightly.

9.00 a.m.

'But it's still a great day,' Anna thinks to herself as she ushers the children into the car and sets off for school. A few jokes on the way ensure a happy and laughter-filled journey so, as this is a **high-vibrational** situation, it speeds up her personal energy field.

9.30 a.m.

The children are safely in school when up strolls Mrs Johnson. 'Oh, no!' Anna says to herself, 'who is she going to be gossiping about today?' Sure enough, away she goes: 'Well, I don't know who she thinks she is ...' and 'What they need a big car like that for I don't know ...'. Now Anna's personal energy field slows down as she lends a sympathetic ear to Mrs Johnson's jealousy, resentment and

Anna's vibrational level is lowered by contact with another person's negative energy.

envy directed at one person after another. The **low-vibrational** conversation drags down Anna's energy field.

10.00 a.m.

The journey home is uneventful; a good thing really, because Anna is now in no mood for any aggravating drivers. At home, the post is waiting.

First, the gas bill: it's slightly more than she was expecting but their budget can cope with it. 'I wonder if we have a gas leak? No, we probably left the heating on more than I realised.' Suddenly **low-vibrational** thoughts begin to creep in, slowing down her energy field.

Next, the electricity bill. That's a lot lower than she expected, which is a nice bonus that makes up for the gas bill. She feels a little uplift, and a small wave of **high-vibrational** joy sweeps in. Up goes her personal energy field.

Next, the credit card statement: not so bad!

But then she opens the telephone bill: £500! 'My goodness, how can that be?' Anxiety takes hold as she scrambles around for the itemised statement. 'I knew it! The internet! I'll swing for him when he gets home!' A flood of **low-vibrational** emotions hit: worry, fear, anger. Anna's personal energy field plummets as she engages in this **low-vibrational** energy. By now, her personal energy field is slowing right down and she feels terrible. That's all she needed; now she has a headache as well.

11.00 a.m.

Anna spends the rest of the morning fretting over her financial problems and feeling very low indeed. 'Will anything ever go right?' she wonders. Suddenly her **low-vibrational** state is interrupted by the doorbell. As she opens the door, Anna is greeted by a big smile from Jane, her next door neighbour. 'Put the kettle on,' says Jane as she charges by, brimming with confidence and **high-**

Anna's vibrational level is raised by contact with another person's positive energy.

vibrational energy. 'You look fed up,' she says, catching Anna's miserable face. 'What's wrong?' Well, that's just what Anna needed and she begins to pour out all her problems. She fires each one towards Jane, who just bats it away with her usual **high-vibrational**, positive outlook. After an hour's conversation, Anna feels decidedly better. Jane's **high-vibrational** attitude has put her problems in perspective, and Anna's personal energy field has shot up. The **low-vibrational** thoughts that weighed heavily on her mind an hour ago now seem trivial, and strangely enough her headache has gone as well. Jane dashes off to her mother's, and Anna decides it's time to do the shopping.

12.00 noon
The sun is bright (although Anna had failed to notice it during her **low-vibrational** morning). Her first stop is the butcher, who is always very friendly. A well-placed compliment pushes up the frequency of her personal energy field, which also has the effect of making her feel good about herself: more **high-vibrational** thoughts, which drown out any regular **low-vibrational** thoughts she normally carries about herself.

12.30 p.m.

Soon the shopping is done, and Anna heads back to the car park, laden down with bags. As she approaches the car, she hears a loud screeching noise heading towards her. She turns to see a car hurtling by at speed. It narrowly misses her, but she drops one of her bags of shopping – eggs, tins and fruit fall everywhere. She is fuming! 'How could that idiot drive like that?' she thinks to herself. 'What if the children had been with me?' Her initial feelings are fear and panic, but they are soon followed by frustration and anger. Anna's heart is pounding at the thought of how close the car came to knocking her down – and not so much as an apology. She decides to report the incident to the police. By this time her personal energy field has plummeted as a result of all this **low-vibrational** energy.

Anna's vibrational level plummets as a result of stress and anger.

2.30 p.m.

After two hours in the police station, Anna is feeling very fed up. The possibility of anything being done about the incident appears to be nil. Anna trudges out. Her personal energy field is now very slow indeed. To compound the situation, she is running late to pick up the children, so she dashes to the school, feeling decidedly down in the dumps. The children are very well behaved on the journey home, as they immediately sense Anna's bad mood. Once in the house, she chases them upstairs to do their homework while she makes the tea, her mind racing with the day's events. Bills, Mrs Johnson's gossiping, the car park incident … Anna wallows in **low-vibrational** thoughts. Her personal energy field is slowing down even further. She feels really depressed. 'Why is life so stressful?' and 'Nothing seems to go right' are the kind of thoughts racing around in her head. The children avoid her, as they can see her bad mood has not lifted. Indeed, Anna's mind is pulsating with anger, which she is ready to direct at her husband when he gets home.

Anna prepares to direct her low-vibrational mood towards her husband.

5.00 p.m.

'Hello, darling!' shouts John, as he opens the front door. Anna is ready for him, fired up and angry, but he stops her dead in her tracks. 'For you,' he says, handing her a dozen red roses. 'I've booked a table at our favourite restaurant to

celebrate my promotion! From now on it's only the best for us. My salary has gone up 20 per cent and they've thrown in a company car. Now, what was it you wanted to say?'
All of a sudden Anna's anger and fear vanish; the good news from her husband has dissipated her negativity. Suddenly, she is feeling good, and her personal energy field races up. 'It was nothing really,' she blurts out. 'Anyway, let's celebrate! What marvellous news!' The children sense that the atmosphere has changed from **low-vibrational** to **high-vibrational** energy. Suddenly the house is filled with happiness; Anna's bad day seems like a distant nightmare. How on earth had she allowed herself to get so down?

7.00 p.m.
A short while later, as she lies soaking in a hot bubble bath with a wonderful night in front of her, Anna thinks back over her day and begins to recognise how she became the victim of her own thinking. Every time she allowed a thought to grab hold of her and control her without offering any resistance, she became the victim of all the **low-vibrational** energy that had come her way. But, she realises, she did not have to engage with these **low-vibrational** energies quite so eagerly. If she could have detached herself from them, her personal energy field would not have been quite so affected. She didn't have to take it so much to heart when Mrs Johnson started resenting and envying everybody. She didn't have to let the bills get her down – she and John had always managed to get by. She didn't need to let the feelings of fear, panic, anger and frustration overwhelm her when the car screeched past her in the car park; and she didn't need to mull over all of the **low-vibrational** incidents for the rest of the afternoon, thus slowing down her personal energy field even further.

Anna's energy field

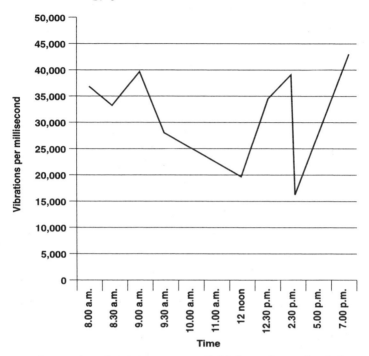

Fluctuations in Anna's energy field throughout the day.

As you can see from the graph, Anna's personal energy field has fluctuated throughout the day as she alternated between positive and negative thoughts – from a low point of 17,000 vibrations per millisecond at 2.30 p.m., when she had just left the police station, to a high point of 48,000 vibrations per millisecond at 7 p.m., as she lay in a hot bath with only positive thoughts in her mind. Remember: the faster our personal energy field vibrates, the better we feel, because we are closer to the high-vibrational energy of love.

Coping with negative energy

It doesn't matter what is pulling you down – the gas bill, the TV breaking down, the children stressing you out. You cannot avoid the low-vibrational energy in your environment; this is the very nature of life. What does matter is how you choose to react to these low-frequency attacks, because you can have some control over how much these situations and events affect you.

I recall an incident in my office in which one of the administrators had had a particularly stressful morning dealing with complaints of various sorts. This low-frequency energy had given her a headache. Then the telephone rang and she found out that she had just won quite a large amount of money. She happily passed on the story of her good fortune to the rest of the staff. A little later, I asked her if she still had a headache. To her amazement, she replied that it had completely disappeared. You see, sometimes even headaches can be instantly cured if you can find a way to lift your personal energy vibration.

On another occasion, a boy I know called Jordan lost his brand-new mobile phone. He was distraught, as his father had just bought him this expensive present. When he realised that he had lost his phone, his whole day looked completely different: one minute he was happy and enjoying himself and the next he was inconsolable. His mind had suddenly become filled with low-vibrational emotions: worry, fear, anger, frustration, disappointment. This had the effect of pulling down his energy frequency. It was several days before Jordan recovered and moved back up to his normal frequency level. That's how powerful negative energy can be.

If negative energy is so powerful, you need an equally powerful weapon to use against it – and that's high-vibrational thinking.

Taking Control

So let's briefly recap. Energy is vibrating all around us. The energy of love is high-vibrational; the energy of fear is low-vibrational. The closer we can stay to the vibration that we call love, the better we will succeed in all aspects of our lives.

Most of life's problems exist at the lower frequency levels, so if you are focused on low-vibrational energy, you are likely to be ill more often, end up in more arguments, have more trouble with your car or your computer, find it harder to get a job or succeed at work and experience problems at school or with the children. In fact, everything will be much more difficult.

High-vibrational thinking is a way of learning to dismiss low-vibrational thoughts and replace them with high-vibrational thoughts. It makes absolute sense to try to think in a more high-vibrational way, because this puts you in control, and being able to control your thoughts and feelings will help you to change your life. You can learn to use HVT in every aspect of your life. You deserve the positive energies of love, happiness and joy in your life just as much as anyone else.

Just being aware of HVT is the first step to taking control of your energy field, as it enables you to understand what is happening in your mind and to appreciate that control is lacking. Once you have taken that first step, it won't be long before you automatically begin to assess situations in terms of energy and put HVT into practice without thinking about it. This makes a welcome change from being controlled by negative energies, being tossed around like a rag doll in the wind.

Reprogramming our subconscious

There are two elements in making HVT work for you: one deals with your fundamental energy levels, and the other deals with how you react to the changing energy levels around you.

The influences we experience during our formative years help to establish our normal vibrational frequency and define our comfort zone: our fundamental feelings about ourselves and the kind of life we believe we deserve. Throughout our life, our subconscious mind monitors our feelings and actions so that we stay within the boundaries of our comfort zone, whether that is good for us or not. If we try to move away from that comfort zone, we are engaging in a battle for control – and it's a battle that we usually lose.

There is another way – one that avoids the battle and enables us to take control. The answer is to reprogramme your subconscious mind and so change the boundaries of your comfort zone.

Let's take the dieting example that we looked at on pages 32–33. While your comfort zone is chips, chips and more chips, any diet will be a huge struggle that is almost doomed to failure, because you will be constantly drawn back to your comfort zone. But if you change the boundaries of your comfort zone, your subconscious mind will monitor what you eat to keep you at the newly programmed weight that is now within your comfort zone. You will be able to change your eating habits, with the result that you are attracted to a more healthy diet of less fattening foods. If you look at those people who have dieted successfully and lost lots of weight permanently, you will generally find that they have also managed to reprogramme their subconscious mind successfully.

If it's improved fitness you are trying to achieve, the principles are just the same. While your comfort zone is an evening with your feet up in front of the TV, that is what your subconscious will be pulling you towards.

HVT is a way of reprogramming that does away with the need for an iron will. This book will show you how to achieve that reprogramming. The first step towards change is to understand how your mind works and accept the power of the subconscious mind. Once you appreciate this, you can begin to move forward and make plans for a new and exciting future.

With HVT you can retrain your inner child.

Of course, once you have reprogrammed your subconscious into a new comfort zone, it will start to form new and more positive habits. If you have an established habit of taking regular exercise, when you miss your exercise for some reason you will feel tired and drained. It's almost as if you are addicted to exercise and without it you feel down. This, again, is your subconscious pushing you to stick to the comfort zone – but in this case, of course, the comfort zone is healthy, so the subconscious is a force for good.

So you can see that your subconscious can be programmed for success or failure, and it will use all its powerful influence to maintain whatever it is programmed for. If we can reprogramme our subconscious for success, clearly this is the answer to many of our problems. This book will show you how to do just that – to change your subconscious comfort zone in relation to the specific problems and issues that are relevant to you.

Start changing now

You don't have to wait until you have read the whole book to make changes in your life. You can start making changes straightaway. Start by dealing with the energy fluctuations you encounter on a daily basis and how you react to them.

Remember the outline of Anna's fairly ordinary day (see pages 44–50). Look at it again and you will see how Anna allowed herself to be engaged by the energies around her, rather than taking control of her own energy field. When she encountered low-vibrational energy from outside, or when her own emotions were low-vibrational – both things we can't always avoid – she allowed herself to be dragged down and ended up feeling even worse. You are probably just the same. Now that you realise that by engaging with low-vibrational thoughts you are only going to damage yourself by dragging down your personal energy field, you can start to implement changes that will make an immediate difference to your life.

Don't engage with low-vibrational energy

The crucial thing is not to engage emotionally with low-vibrational energy, because it is when you become emotionally attached to negativity that you are most damaged. Your personal energy frequency will plummet and move you into a much more difficult frequency zone.

You can now recognise low-vibrational energy as anything that pulls you down and makes you feel negative: anger, disappointment, envy, spite and so on. When you encounter that kind of energy, the secret is to remain calm and to let the negative energy pass over you without buying into it. Try to visualise the energy moving away from you and disappearing, rather than hanging on to it and engaging with it mentally. The principle is very simple: recognise it and reject it.

Start right now. The next time you find low-vibrational thoughts coming into your mind, let them go. You almost certainly won't succeed straightaway; it will take a little practice, but even the first time you try it, you will feel some impact. Then, every time you succeed, it will become easier and more automatic to reject negativity. If you stick at it and follow the specific guidance in this book, you will get better at it every day.

Take bills as an example. If you have a gas bill that is higher than you expected, you obviously have to do something about it. But worrying is not going to make the bill any smaller; nor is it going to get it paid. If you put aside the worry, you have more energy to think about positive things that will help you to solve the actual problem of paying the bill. Your mind will be able to focus on the options: you can dip into your savings, contact the supplier and arrange to pay it off gradually, turn down the heating thermostat so it doesn't happen again – or whatever.

Concentrate on the present

So visualising negative energy draining away will help. Another very simple way to handle low-vibrational thought patterns is to concentrate on the present.

We all spend too much of our time thinking about the past or the future. Our minds tend to dwell on something that has happened or something that might happen until this becomes a habit that is difficult to break. In fact, we are often scarcely aware that we are doing this.

It is all too easy to dwell on a low-vibrational event that has happened in the past: the time we struggled to meet a payment date; the time someone shouted at us or let us down. We keep running it over and over again in our minds like some kind of looped tape action replay. The result of replaying thoughts of anger, frustration, disappointment, fear or uncertainty is that our personal frequency level is dragged down even more, draining away positive energy.

Likewise, we may focus our attention on a future negative event that may never happen: the cold we are sure we are going to catch, the redundancy that is bound to come, and so on. Similarly, the effect is to lower our frequency level, leaching away all our positive energy.

The past is gone and we cannot change it. Dwelling on its negative energies will only drag us down. We simply need to learn from it and move on. The future is not here yet; worrying about something that may or may not happen will only drag down your personal energy field, making life much harder in the process.

If you can avoid this time trap and think in the present, you will find that your energy levels remain high. By being alert to this pitfall, you can train your mind to recognise when you are about to fall into the trap. Then you simply stop and remind yourself to concentrate on the present. If you have a problem, look at what you can do now to solve it in the best possible way.

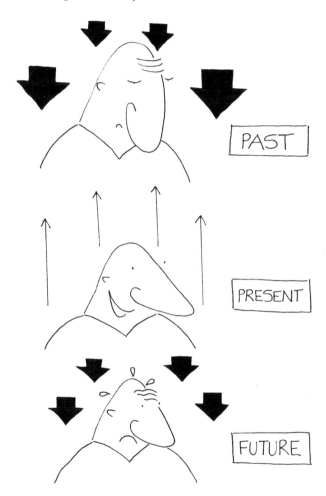

Dwelling on the past and worrying about the future is a waste of energy. Stay focused in the present if you want to get the best out of your life.

Use high-vibrational thinking to clear your mind of clutter and stay focused in the present moment; then you are ready to handle life to the best of your ability.

Take one step at a time

There will be times when you don't manage to dismiss low-vibrational thoughts altogether. Don't worry about it – for worrying is in itself hanging on to low-vibrational energies. Look at what you did achieve; tell yourself how much better you did it than last time; congratulate yourself and move on. Before long you will find that you are more and more in control. This means that your personal energy field will not slow down as easily next time you encounter low-vibrational energy, and you won't have to spend every day on a mental rollercoaster ride.

Remember, you are more in control than you realise. Your thoughts create your reality, so if you fill your mind with high-vibrational thoughts, you will have a more positive, enjoyable and fulfilling life. You can take control of your own energy.

How HVT Relates to Depression

You can see how HVT relates to depression if you look at life in terms of what 'energy zone' you are currently in, which means thinking of things in terms of energy. Imagine there are three zones: high zone, mid zone and low zone; how you are feeling determines which zone you exist in.

High zone

When we feel happy and on top of the world (maybe when we have just finished work and are getting ready for an exciting night out or about to set off for a two-week holiday in the sun), we could say this is when we are in the high zone. This is when our energy field is vibrating at a fast rate and we have high-vibrational thoughts racing around in our mind. Negativity is not really affecting us and we feel great.

Mid zone

This is when we are more than likely in what is considered our 'normal' state and our mind ticks over with various positive and negative situations that we face every day of our lives. This is where most of us spend most of our time and it is regarded as normal to exist at this vibrational level.

Low zone

This is a much more negative place and this is when we are predominantly negative in our thought patterns about ourselves and the world around us. It's these low-vibrational thoughts that hold down the vibration of our energy field and keep us held down in the low zone.

I believe what we call depression is in fact just another name for 'low vibration', as the feelings associated with depression are exactly the same as the symptoms you experience when in the low zone. This is somewhere that we will all probably visit during our lives and more than

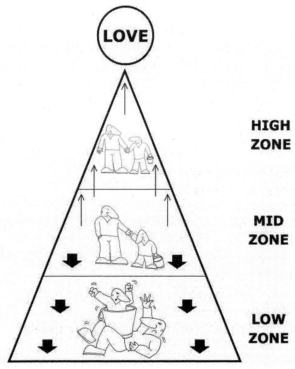

The more insecurities we have the more we will be pulled down by them, which could result in us being dragged into the low zone and suffering from depression.

likely on many occasions. Anything can be the catalyst: an argument with our partner, an unexpected bill, worry about our school exams, a speeding fine, a pending court case, financial difficulties, losing our job, worrying over a loved one; the list goes on. When most of us plunge into the low zone we rise back up just as quickly, once the problem that dragged us down has been dealt with. Sometimes just a good night's sleep is sufficient to put things into perspective and make us realise we were just caught up in the negative situation.

The difference between a quick visit to the low zone and depression is that for the depressed person it is *not* a quick visit. They become stuck there for a long period of time. It's in the low zone where all the low-vibrational stuff exists: hate, greed, self-doubt, self-loathing, fear, pain, selfishness, resentment, anger, cruelty, illness... So, if we spend a lot of time down there we are going to be surrounded by this negativity and we will soon pick up the pain and suffering that goes hand in hand with this state of mind. When you are in the high zone you don't have the negative symptoms that are prevalent in the low zone. These might be:

▸ Tiredness and loss of energy
▸ Persistent sadness
▸ Physical aches and pains
▸ Sleeping problems – difficulties getting off to sleep or waking up much earlier than usual
▸ Loss of appetite
▸ Loss of sex drive and/or sexual problems
▸ Loss of self-confidence and self-esteem
▸ Difficulty concentrating
▸ Not being able to enjoy things that are usually pleasurable or interesting
▸ Undue feelings of guilt or worthlessness
▸ Feelings of helplessness and hopelessness
▸ Avoiding other people, sometimes even your close friends

- ▸ Finding it hard to function at work/college/school
- ▸ Thinking about suicide and death
- ▸ Self-harm

Many of these are also the symptoms associated with depression, which is often described as feeling like a weight is pushing down on your head. In fact, it's all of the negative thoughts forcing you down into the low zone.

Who Gets Depression?

Depression is something that I believe 99.9 per cent of us are suffering from all of the time, but we only regard it as an illness when it gets to a certain stage.

If you refer back to our potential as a human being, then you can see that our natural state would be to vibrate at the frequency of love and attain what is called enlightenment. Anything less than this means we are affected by some amount of negativity. This means, since 99.9 per cent of us are not in a state of enlightenment, that we are in fact in a state of depression. The intensity of this varies, of course, all the way down to the levels where we start to malfunction seriously (the low zone).

Severe depression, that is, depression at levels at which it can be considered an illness, affects people from all walks of life. Well-known people that have suffered include Sigmund Freud, Marilyn Monroe, Abraham Lincoln, Isaac Newton, Jean-Claude Van Damme, Ilie Nastase, Ernest Hemingway, Ray Charles: the list goes on and on. Severe depression knows no boundaries and it is an illness that can touch any of us at some time in our lives.

Depression is the most common mental illness, affecting one in five people at some point in their lives, with twice as many women as men being affected. Only 20 per cent of sufferers seek treatment, and yet up to 90 per cent of people respond positively to treatment.

In a world made of energy it is difficult to avoid, yet if handled properly it can present a wonderful opportunity for personal growth.

What Does Depression Feel Like?

There are different types of depression and different people experience it in different ways. You might feel any of the following.

When you are depressed you feel strangely subdued and unable to focus on anything properly. Your mind seems to drift off and you find it increasingly difficult to concentrate on even the simplest tasks. You have no energy to do anything and your body feels tired and drained. You can for a while force yourself to deal with everyday tasks, but it seems impossible to maintain your concentration. Tiredness sweeps over you and you long to close your eyes and drift off to sleep to give you relief from this feeling of numbness.

You go cold on your loved ones and unconsciously push them away with your words and actions. You are a different person and behave in a way that is not the usual you. Even if you try to act normally, it seems that you can't quite be your usual self and you struggle to maintain any consistency. Sometimes your pain can become so severe that your whole insides seem to hurt and you look to blame anybody for your plight. This is when your loved ones can bear the brunt and you lash out, somehow convincing yourself that it is their fault that you hurt so much. Relationships can suffer irreparable damage.

You may have emotional outbursts ranging from terrible shows of anger to tearful weeping periods when you feel helpless and too weak to cope. You may even feel that you could harm yourself as a sudden rush of despair sweeps over you and in very bad moments you may even have suicidal thoughts, as you desperately seek release from this nightmare. You may even feel a strange underlying sense of happiness drift over you, as you go through this agony; it's as if you are somewhere deep down inside of you actually enjoying the pain. I believe this is your inner child showing its contentment at keeping you within the confines of your comfort zone; your inner child will be happy doing this even if you are not.

On the physical level you could experience headaches and other unusual aches and pains for no apparent reason. You might feel like lashing out at other people even to the point of causing them physical harm and your desperate desire to feel better could even turn you into a bully.

Types of Depression

Several different types of depression have been identified by the medical profession. You might have heard the terms dysthymic disorder, endogenous depression, manic depression, bipolar disorder, seasonal affective disorder and post-natal depression, for example. Their causes and symptoms vary and there can be vastly differing individual responses.

Major depression

Major depression may be something that creeps up on you over a number of years, as though you have slowly slid into it over a period of time; or it could be caused by a traumatic event in your life.

Some people are thrust into a major depression due to a life crisis, such as the death of a loved one or the break-up of a relationship, but after successful treatment they never have depression again. For others, the depression might recur throughout their lives as they encounter other traumas. The road to recovery can be longer when there has been a slow, gradual descent into depression over a long period of time. You become used to this very negative state of mind and the longer you leave it without treatment, the harder it will be to get out of. It will have become your comfort zone.

Depression can have a negative affect on all areas of a person's life, making it difficult to function properly and making it difficult for family and friends. Everybody handles depression in their own way and some people can still carry on their day-to-day business, working and dealing with responsibilities to a degree, but others can be totally disabled by the condition. It is thought that half of all suicides are due to depression.

Milder depression

A milder but longer lasting form of depression can leave sufferers in a daily depressed state. Most people in this state manage to get on with their lives and often don't even know they are depressed, although the symptoms are severe enough to cause distress and interfere with normal life. It's a case of just going through the motions without any real enthusiasm or interest. You don't seem able to enjoy anything, even if it's something that you enjoyed before. Being a chronic condition means people close to you think that this is simply your nature and your personality, not actually realising that there is something wrong. You are at risk of developing major depression and many sufferers often experience this. This type of person is often regarded as being negative and pessimistic always seeing the down side.

Seasonal affective disorder

Seasonal affective disorder (SAD) is thought to be brought on by seasonal changes. Lack of sunlight is thought to be the main cause of this disorder, a theory borne out by an increasing number of cases in the northern hemisphere.

Exactly what causes this seasonal reaction is not clearly understood and there is still some debate about whether it is biological or psychological in origin. It may be that SAD is not a psychological disorder in itself, but an exaggeration of other forms of depression that are already present. It seems to affect younger people more than older people. It is also more likely to affect women than men.

Symptoms of depression are not usually as severe as with a major depression and tend to disappear in the spring. It is possible that people who suffer from this form of depression are affected as the dark nights draw in, hence the connection with lack of sunlight.

If you suffer from SAD, you might lack energy and need much more sleep than usual. Sufferers often crave carbohydrates and can be prone to putting on weight.

Post-natal depression

This form of depression affects between 10 per cent and 20 per cent of new mothers and it often develop slowly two to three weeks after giving birth. Symptoms can include panic attacks, feelings of inadequacy, sleeping difficulties, fears of dying and being unable to cope. It may be difficult to spot because it creeps up slowly, making it difficult to diagnose. The severity of this form of depression varies. Half of all mothers suffer to some degree from the so-called 'baby blues', usually within a few days of the baby's birth. This can take the form of crying all day or being very anxious about things large and small, feeling very touchy about things and prone to anger over minor incidents. For most new mums these feelings don't last long and generally disappear after a few days.

For some mothers, however, this develops into post-natal depression, which is more severe and long lasting, perhaps even as long as four or five years. Symptoms include:

‣ Lots of crying often about small things
‣ Panic attacks
‣ Self-loathing
‣ Underlying feeling of fear for no apparent reason

- Bouts of anger and irritability
- Disturbing thoughts about your health and that of your baby
- Hating your partner
- Hating your baby
- Fear of hurting your baby
- Self-doubt
- Low confidence
- Temper tantrums
- Not sleeping very well
- An overall feeling of being unable to cope
- Lack of sex drive
- Fear of being alone
- Doubt in your skills as a mother

This kind of negative thinking also often places stress on relationships and can even result in break-ups.

What Causes Depression?

Understanding HVT gives us the ability to view depression in a whole new and very revealing way. We can now see that being depressed is, in fact, just another way of saying that our personal energy field is down in the low zone. The fact that we are vibrating slowly and have slid down the vibrational scale opens us up to experiencing all the low-vibrational thoughts and feelings that exist down there. The further down that we are, the worse it feels, and this is the basic difference between the identified forms of depression.

Easy to understand

This new understanding of depression is incredibly empowering and enables us to analyse more easily what has caused it in the first place. We need to find out what has caused the drop in vibration of our energy field and make the necessary adjustments to bring us back to our normal level. To do this, we first have a look at how our energy field is programmed to be at its normal level.

Jeff and Dave

Referring back to the example that we used of Jeff and Dave's life (see page 35), we can see that our normal vibrational level is largely determined by our upbringing. It's mainly during these early years that we pick up our negative thought patterns about ourselves and the world around us. The degree and intensity of these thought patterns dictates where our normal vibrational level will be. I refer to these negative thoughts as our personal insecurities, so let's take a closer look at how this works.

Personal insecurities

Every one of us carries our own low-vibrational thought patterns about ourselves, and these negative thoughts hold down the vibration of our personal energy field. As we saw in the lives of Jeff and Dave, these negative thoughts can be very damaging to every area of our lives. If you can imagine a large metal bucket full of all the low-vibrational

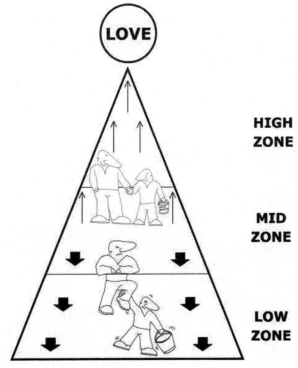

The heavier the bucket of insecurities that your inner child is holding on to, the further down you will be pulled.

thoughts that you habitually carry about yourself and the world around you, then you can see how this acts as a dead weight holding you down and preventing your energy vibration from rising. This bucket full of negativity can be extremely damaging to you, keeping you held down at your normal vibration level. If you can imagine your inner child (subconscious mind) holding on to the bucket with a tight grip, then you can now see clearly where within your mind this bucket full of insecurities can be found. It resides in the programme by which your inner child runs your life, the programme that was mainly put in place during the first five or six years of your life.

Negatives in life pull down your vibration

When you were born you will have had very few insecurities about yourself. Then, as your life goes on, you gather negative opinions about yourself, as you encounter the ups and downs of life. Of course, these ups and downs are unavoidable, but your upbringing determines just how severe your insecurities will be.

Let's say your parents never showed you any affection, never cuddled or kissed you, then it would be no surprise if you grew up feeling unloved. This would become your programming and when later on in life you did receive love (high-vibrational energy), you would find this very difficult to accept. This would result in your inner child trying to pull you away from this source of love, trying to keep you down at the vibrational frequency at which it was programmed to believe you belong.

Many scenarios can add to your bucket

Maybe you felt that your sister or brother received more attention than you did, which resulted in you as a child becoming envious. This pattern of envy can be carried right throughout your life, ready to surface at any time, which can be very damaging to you.

There are many scenarios that can occur and there are many other influential factors that have a bearing on determining your insecurities and the intensity of them. Your personality type, your genes and your temperament all affect how you react to situations; we could all have exactly the same upbringing but come out with different levels of insecurity.

We can add more weight to our bucket as we go along

You can also pick up insecurities from your relationships. For example, if you have a bad experience with a habitually unfaithful partner, this would add to your insecurities. This could make you very insecure with a new partner, as your trust has previously been shattered. The fact that your past partner was unfaithful may well make you feel you are not deserving of love, because you interpret their continual inconstancy as a sign that they preferred somebody else to you. This can be very damaging to your self-esteem and result in you taking on board this negative programming. This adds to your bucket of insecurities, making it even heavier.

It's how we see ourselves

Basically, an insecurity is a negative way that we view ourselves, which affirms to us that we are not deserving of love. How many insecurities we have and their intensity determines how far we will hold our personal energy vibration rate below the vibration of love. The heavier the bucket, the more it will pull you down. If you can imagine your bucket is 25 per cent full of insecurities about yourself, then the bucket will pull you down to loving yourself 75 per cent. The heavier your bucket, the more you will live your life through the insecurities contained within it.

In a worst case scenario you could end up living your entire life through the insecurities contained within your bucket. This means living full time with feelings such as worthlessness, fear, self-hate, jealousy, resentment and envy, and these extremely negative and damaging thought patterns could become your everyday mantra. Some people spend their lives in this state and this is a very low-vibrational zone. This is the zone of major depression.

Our normal level determines how prone to depression we are

Fortunately most of us don't have that heavy a bucket, which means that our insecurities will only occasionally engulf us and drag us into the low zone. Most of the time we can go through life without even realising that they are there, happily existing in the mid zone. Then one day, and often through a trivial action, they can be triggered off.

If we are very well balanced and feel good about ourselves, our normal vibration level will be quite high, which means we will be less likely to be affected by depression. If our bucket is a little heavier and our normal level is low down in the mid zone, we could easily become susceptible to depression. You see, it's not so far to go to be in the low zone. Any particularly negative incident could activate your insecurities and the associated negative thoughts could tip you into the low zone: you suffer from major depression. With this in mind, Jeff would be more likely to suffer from some form of depression than Dave, because in energy terms Jeff's life is being lived closer to the low zone, due to his more negative state of mind.

Other negative influences

Negativity attacks our energy field through many other sources. The media is a constant source of bad news, war, murder, crime, rape, violence, death and mayhem, projected at us on a daily basis through TV, newspapers and radio. This is a major contributor to damaging our energy field and you would be amazed at how much better you would feel without this dragging you down everyday. Computer games and movies are also often full of very negative images and incidents. It seems we are been bombarded by low-vibrational energy from all angles. Everywhere we turn it is there. If you have a fairly low-vibrational energy field you are more susceptible to experiencing some form of depression when you are subjected to this constant bombardment. Watching a movie filled with murder, aggression or violence can trigger off your thoughts, bringing other similar negative situations to mind. This fills you with negativity and drags down your vibration.

Bullying, too, can push you down into depression, as it can fill you with fear and self doubt.

Depression and the over 65s

Depression affects four times as many people over the age of 65 as in other age groups.

When you get to the later stages of your life lots of important things that took up your time may no longer be there. You probably no longer work. Your children will now have their own lives and no longer need you as much. You will have lots more time on your hands. You may feel after a lifetime of responsibilities that you have no purpose and you are no longer needed by anyone. You may not be as fit and healthy as you used to be and might suffer from some sort of physical ailment. All of these things can very easily generate negative thoughts and cause a drop in vibration. It's perfectly natural to feel this way and very easy to let this line of thought pull you down into depression. You need to renew your sense of purpose in order to keep up your vibration levels (see page 86).

Treating Depression

There are many ways to treat depression and you should seek professional help if you feel overwhelmed by your symptoms. Whether you go for conventional medical help or seek a holistic approach through complementary therapies is a matter of choice. Many people benefit from a combination of medication and counselling. The important thing is that you do something.

Your GP or other medical professional might suggest a course of cognitive behaviour therapy, a method of dealing with the underlying negative thoughts that are conducive to low moods and the consequent behaviour associated with depression. Alternatively, psychotherapy is aimed at dealing with past negative incidents that may be the root cause of the depression. This requires lots of commitment and time for the client and the therapist.

Drug treatment can be used to restore the imbalance of brain chemicals that plays a part in major depression. Talk with your GP about whether this is appropriate for you. They may feel that a course of treatment will help to stabilise the chemical imbalance you are experiencing. This should enable you to see your problems in perspective and give you the ability to begin to cope with them and find solutions. It is not weakness if you need medical help for a time. Your body is affected as well as your emotions and in some cases this may be essential. It does not necessarily mean you will have to continue to take medication in the long term.

How HVT can help

Looking at depression using HVT opens up a whole new way of looking at the problem. Seeing the world in terms of energy makes depression easier to understand and enables us to see what is really happening. The obvious answer to beating depression is to increase the vibration of our personal energy field on a permanent basis. This means we have to get rid of – or at least make lighter – our bucket of insecurities, which is done by reprogramming our subconscious mind. We must change negative thought patterns for positive thought patterns.

Our bucket of insecurities resides in the programming that our inner child carries, so this is where our focus must be. The three steps to a depression-free life at the end of this book take you through a six-week course to reprogramme.

HVT Applied to Depression

As discussed earlier (see page 69), depression can take different forms and its symptoms and treatment vary between individuals.

Major depression

The severest form of depression drags you well down into the low zone and your thoughts are so negative that you just can't get out. You feel as though you are living in the darkness, crushed by the weight of negativity in your mind.

If you have slid here over a long period of time, the negative thought patterns may have become so embedded within your mind that you will need lots of time and treatment to pull yourself back up. You need to deal with lots of life issues to believe in yourself again and realise that you are deserving of love (high-vibrational energy) in your life. If you have been thrust here by a traumatic event then you need to deal with the negativity that has been generated in order for you to rise back up. It could be something like the death of a loved one or maybe a serious accident that has dragged you into the depths. In this case, the negative thought patterns generated are new and have had less time to become ingrained in your thinking process.

Milder depression

In terms of HVT, milder depression means that you are in the low zone but not as far down as you would be with major depression. If you let your energy levels slip further, your depression will become more serious.

Seasonal affective disorder

Every person has their own energy field, which in a collective situation becomes part of the collective energy field. This applies to any type of group, be it a team, a town, a city, the workplace, a family or a school. I am sure we all have our favourite places and towns that we like to visit and I am also sure we all have places that we don't like, which somehow feel down and uncomfortable. I believe we are sensing the collective energy of the people that are present and if it is high we like it and if it is low we don't.

Have you noticed how nice it feels at Christmas when for a few days everything seems to have a different, lovely feel to it? I believe this is due to a rise in vibration of the collective energy field that we are feeling, as for a short while everybody puts aside their problems and worries and gets ready for a nice Christmas. (It only happens once a year, but how great it would be if we could all learn to think differently and keep up this spirit all year round.) After the high of Christmas, we get the down period of January and February, as we all start back with our negative thinking: worry about overspending at Christmas, having to go back to work and, for those of us in the north, the cold weather and dark nights. SAD is possibly at its peak after Christmas, as people susceptible to it are dragged down those extra few vibrations by the collective energy field. It affects all of us, but the people that are hovering just above the low zone in their normal state are the ones that will experience it as depression.

Post-natal depression

After giving birth to a child a mother faces many challenging thoughts and fears that may have an adverse effect on her energy field. These negative thoughts are what I believe pull down her vibration and in some cases pull her far enough down to experience post-natal depression.

It is perhaps not surprising if after having carried a child in the womb for nine months, nurturing and caring for it, a woman feels a negative impact when suddenly this very real part of her no longer exists within her. She might even pick up on the baby's feelings and emotions, as it is suddenly thrust into this new, bright, cold and noisy world, when up to this point all it has known is the warmth and security of its mother's womb. It would be natural for the baby to be frightened and disorientated, as it settles into this new environment. There is no closer bond than a mother and child and it would be perfectly normal for the mother to feel the baby's fears.

Other obvious thoughts come into play as the first few hours and then days go by: 'Will I be able to cope?', 'Can I really handle the responsibility of a newborn baby?', 'What is this going to do to my life?', 'I will never just have myself to look out for again,', 'Can I afford the expense of a baby?', 'What if my child is harmed?', 'What kind of world have I brought my child into?'. These thoughts can create fear and self-doubt within a mother's mind and lead to a fall in her energy vibration rate if she is not careful. Most new mothers will experience this to some degree, but for some it will lead to depression, which can be long lasting and damaging. As the first few months pass by these negative thought patterns can be added to, as the new mother finds her life turned upside down and she has to endure sleepless nights.

The demands of a newborn baby can be very difficult to cope with. Thoughts of anger, frustration, worry, restriction and resentment can take their toll and a mother's energy vibration will suffer from this cloud of negativity gripping hold of her mind. This is why post-natal depression often (though not exclusively) affects mothers who have a history of depression. It's all that's needed to tip them back down the vibrational scale.

The HVT Inner Child Theory

If we consider that our subconscious programming is the predominant factor in determining our average vibrational level, then this is what we must change, in order to deal with depression of whatever type that we may be suffering. To alter our programming in a positive way will move us up the vibrational scale and help to eradicate depression. Viewing our subconscious mind as our inner child makes this easier to understand.

Somebody suffering from major depression may have an inner child that is very gloomy and sad. This very negative inner child acts as an anchor firmly holding them down in the low-vibrational zone, just like mine did when my father died.

My experience of bereavement
Losing a loved one is something most of us have to face at sometime in our lives. We go through the grieving process and this can take months or even years, but what we often overlook is that the constant pain inside of us is actually our inner child upset and sobbing. The whole healing process seems to neglect this and we spend all of our time giving attention to our adult self (conscious mind) and more often than not we totally ignore our inner child.

Remember that your inner child is exactly that: a five-year-old. Just imagine yourself at five years old living inside of you. When a loved one dies, how can you expect a child to understand what has happened? You must take time and explain to your inner child what has happened and you do this through visualisation (see page 111).

When my father died, I was 37 years old and well aware of what it felt like to lose somebody, so I thought I would be able to cope and get on with my life. Initially, I was understandably upset and hurt by his death, but I fully expected this gloom to pass, as I needed to get on with my life.

But after a few months I began to realise that I had become withdrawn and non-communicative. I would sit in silence while others chatted away around me. This felt like I was going backwards in terms of self-development and confidence, and I started to worry about my situation. I decided to seek help and read a number of books on coping with the death of a parent, but to no avail. I even attended a one-day workshop to deal with bereavement, but although a felt a slight lift, within hours I soon fell back into my depression. Another month or two passed and I was becoming desperate, as I could not seem to pull out of the depression that engulfed me.

Then one Sunday morning, I was flicking through a book about psychology and I came across a chapter entitled 'The Inner Child'. This was the first time I had heard of the inner child and I read with great interest. Then it dawned on me: it was my inner child that was causing me all of these problems. He was upset and crying at the loss of his dad and nobody even knew he was there. I realised that I had been giving all of my attention to the adult me (conscious mind) and done nothing whatsoever to help the inner child in me (subconscious mind). I immediately began to do a visualisation exercise to comfort my inner child. I explained to him that I loved him very much and I would take care of him now. I even brought my dad into the exercise to reassure him that he was going to be okay.

I couldn't believe what had taken place; months of depression were cured in 10 minutes. I got up from the bed and I felt absolutely fine. It was the most astonishing thing that I had ever experienced and from that moment on I knew how important it was to comfort the inner child. Mine had been engulfed by low-vibrational thoughts of hurt, sorrow, fear and pain, and it was his thoughts and feelings that had kept me depressed and stuck in the low frequency zone for months. I, the adult me, felt fine, but I couldn't rise back up the frequency scale because of the negative thoughts in the mind of my inner child. When I didn't understand what was happening to me, I had no control at all. It was only when I realised that I had an inner child and carried out the comfort visualisation, that I was able to release myself from the nightmare. The hurt and pain that I had been carrying inside me was simply a very upset and neglected child.

The inner child and forms of depression

A mother suffering from post-natal depression may have a jealous inner child that feels rejected at the arrival of the newborn baby. Just like a five-year-old might feel when a new brother or sister arrives on the scene, suddenly somebody else is getting all the attention. This can create negative feelings within the inner child's mind, which pulls down the vibration of the mother's energy field. Or maybe the inner child is full of fear and trepidation at the thought of such a huge life change, which may even threaten the boundaries of its comfort zone.

Big changes in our lives are so stressful because they trigger off panic and fear within our inner child. Your inner child will kick and scream if you do anything that threatens to move it out of its comfort zone.

Seasonal affective disorder may well be brought on by lack of sunlight, because I think we all know how much better we feel when the sun is shining. I am sure we feel replenished and energised by sunlight, as the cells of our physical body respond to the sun's powerful rays. I think we also know that a child confined to the house during the cold winter months soon gets bored and gloomy. Then the sun shines and off goes the child full of joy and excitement at being able to play outside. Maybe this is how our inner child reacts, hence the dragging down of our vibration rate in the cold, bleak winter months.

If we consider that the source of our depression lies in the attitude and state of mind of our inner child, then we can see that improving how our inner child feels can help us to relieve the symptoms of depression. We must convince our inner child that we love them and that they deserve love (high-vibrational energy) in their life. The happier and more loved we can make our inner child feel, the better and more deserving of love we will also feel. This will change our whole life as everything runs much more smoothly in the higher vibrational zones. The happier our inner child feels the lighter our bucket of insecurities will be and therefore pull us down the vibrational scale less.

How To Beat Depression

If you want to apply the theories of HVT to relieving depression, you must raise the vibration of your energy field on a permanent and long-lasting basis. You must believe that you deserve love in your life and there are a number of things that you can do to achieve this.

Later I will take you through my 'Three steps to a depression-free life', designed to effect permanent change to how you think about yourself and the world around you. First, though, let's consider what you could do to lift your energy into a higher zone.

Diet

What you eat is a major contributor to the vibration of your energy field. Food that our world provides naturally, such as raw fruit and vegetables, grains and nuts, is very good for you and full of energy and goodness. Eating too many processed foods can have an adverse affect on your energy field. It is all too easy to eat too many fast, convenience foods, which damage your vibration level and deplete your energy, making you feel tired and drained.

Drinking water is essential for the correct functioning of your body and helps give you energy and cleanse your system of toxins.

Don't engage in the struggle

Life throws many challenges our way and we are presented on a daily basis with many different life situations. These challenges could be anything: financial problems, health issues, relationship breakdowns, anti-social behaviour, bullying, the car breaking down or our children being upset. These types of negative incidents are commonplace and part and parcel of life on our planet. The problem is that if we allow ourselves to be engaged by them, things can become very difficult indeed.

It's very easy to be drawn in and very difficult to remain unaffected. When we engage in this type of negative situation we are simply allowing ourselves to be dragged down. Thoughts and feelings of frustration, anger, bitterness or worry do nothing but cause us harm. We would be more proficient at handling these problems if we could remain unaffected and at a higher vibrational level.

To engage in the struggle that life constantly presents us with is futile and simply exaggerates the particular problem that has caused the negativity in the first place. You must deal with life's problems without letting them drag you down in order to prevent damage to the vibration of your energy field. You must be aware when negativity attempts to ensnare you and remain detached from it, whilst dealing with the situation. It takes a little practice at first, but now you understand about how energy levels work you should work towards keeping your energy at a higher vibrational level and away from the low zone that could result in depression.

Other people will also be quite happy to draw you into their dramas, so you need to learn to remain detached in these situations.

Make a positive action plan

Here are some ideas that might help you to feel better about yourself and so raise you into a higher energy zone. Don't set yourself impossible targets, though. It's better to start with one small thing a day. The objective here is to implement life changes that will have a positive effect on your thinking process. So, make yourself a positive action plan, and decide the changes you are going to make and tick them off as you achieve them.

Get physical

Try to take some exercise every day. It will lift your mood and give you a sense of achievement. You could take up jogging or join a gym, go swimming, cycling or horse riding. Spend more time in nature by walking in the countryside or your local park, or go for a paddle in the sea. Take your dog for a walk (or borrow a friend's).

Get out of the house

Don't let yourself become isolated. Join a club or get involved with a group that interests you. Volunteer for charity work, which will help keep you busy and stave off those negative thoughts.

Develop your sense of purpose

Having a focus in your life helps raise your self-esteem. Get a job, go back to college and do that course you've always promised yourself, or become active in your local community: join the parish council, for example.

Instil some order

Have a clear out. It's very therapeutic to remove the physical clutter from your life. Then put your financial affairs in order. Take a look at your wardrobe and make an effort with your appearance. Clear out mental clutter, too, by apologising to anybody you feel you may have wronged in the past. Make up with family and friends you may have fallen out with.

Avoid negativity

Replace bad habits with good ones. Drink less alcohol and stop smoking. Try to read fewer newspapers; read inspirational books instead. Watch less TV and be selective; avoid particularly negative programmes. Try to do one good deed everyday.

Learn to relax

Work on reducing your stress levels. Take up yoga or join a meditation group. Buy a relaxation tape or treat yourself to an aromatherapy massage.

And more besides

I am sure there are many other things you can think of that would make you feel better; just add them to the list. The point is we are looking to make very positive changes to your life and this will help raise your opinion of yourself, which in turn will push up the vibration of your energy field. You need to get into new routines so your life takes a new direction and you leave your old negative life behind. Without the knowledge of HVT it is very difficult in this world of ours not to be affected by negativity and it's no surprise that so many of us experience depression at some point in our lives. I know I have experienced it on many occasions and it is only since discovering HVT that I have been able to have an element of control. I still feel depression creeping up on me sometimes but I now know how to banish those negative thoughts and rise back up the vibrational scale.

Your Potential

'**W**e are unlimited beings,
experiencing life in a physical
body subject to the ceilings of our imagination.' Bill Hicks

Your potential is to attune your personal energy field to the
frequency of love, on a permanent basis. This is the true
goal of life, which we are all fully engaged in pursuing,
whether we realise it or not. Everything that we do is
centred on this one ultimate focus; our whole lives are
geared towards this deep-seated desire to be at one with the
energy that we call love. To achieve this would be the end
to all misery and unhappiness in our lives. Never again
would we sink to the depths of despair, as we would be
vibrating at a frequency where such low-frequency feelings
and emotions could not exist. To achieve this goal is, of
course, very rare indeed, but nevertheless it is the key to
achieving the goal that we call happiness.

Amazing experience
A number of years ago I had an amazing experience. I was
going through a particularly stressful time, as we all do
from time to time. I remember feeling very down and
desperately searching for an answer to my problems – just
the usual problems that we all encounter, of course, but
which can sometimes seem huge and insurmountable. I
found it difficult to sleep and remember mulling things

over in my mind, but eventually I fell into a deep sleep.

The next thing I knew, the sun was shining through the blinds and I could hear the birds singing. For some completely inexplicable reason I felt absolutely great and on top of the world, and the huge problems that had so engulfed me the previous evening now seemed trivial. I had never felt better in my life and I set off to work in an almost dream-like trance as the world had taken on a whole new and exciting persona. Everything looked different to me. The grass was greener than I had ever noticed it before, the sky was an incredible blue, somehow brighter and deeper than I had ever seen it. When I got to work the amazement continued. Every person that I encountered appeared to have bright shining eyes, as if some kind of energy was pouring out from deep within their being. Their faces were shining with joy and they all looked so beautiful and I remember feeling such compassion for everybody. It was almost like I wanted to take care of everybody and look after them.

This incredible feeling lasted for about one month and it is an experience that I will never forget. I was so disappointed when my old feelings slowly reappeared. I tried desperately to cling on to this amazing and beautiful feeling of unconditional love that I had inexplicably come across, but unfortunately the real world came back and reclaimed me. At the time I never fully appreciated or understood what had actually taken place, I just knew something quite profound had happened to me. It was almost impossible to explain my experience to other people, as with my lack of real understanding it was difficult to put into words. So I simply pushed this amazing experience to the back of my mind.

It wasn't until some years later, as my understanding of HVT grew, that I actually appreciated what had really taken place. Somehow, for one month of my life I had come close to resonating at the same frequency as the energy that we call love. I don't know why this happened to me: I just know that it did. This incredible experience gave me a new life goal, to get that feeling back, and it was HVT that gave me the understanding of how to achieve that. It all fell into place. I had surely found the true answer to the holy grail of life, the search for happiness, and it was all to do with energy.

A glimpse of enlightenment

My feelings now about that amazing month of my life are that I had experienced what it must feel like to attain what we refer to as enlightenment. This of course is the ultimate goal of many a seeker of wisdom and happiness and you will find reference to this in many books and teachings. My personal view of enlightenment now is that to attain enlightenment you must reach a state of being where you have no low-vibrational thoughts or feelings within your mind. You are so free of negativity that your personal energy field rises accordingly and you bask in the frequency of love.

As I look back on that time, I feel I have now come to a clear understanding of what actually happened. The stress and pressure that I felt at that time had somehow triggered off a reaction in my mind. This reaction had let go of all of the low-vibrational thoughts and feelings that I was carrying and allowed my personal energy frequency to rise. This releasing of negativity from within my mind allowed my vibration to hit the heights and I was able to resonate closer to the frequency of love than I had ever been before. The feeling was indescribably beautiful and on reflection I now realise that this is what we are all really seeking. The only thing holding us back from this is the low-vibrational thoughts and feelings that we constantly carry in our minds. It's simple. Take the low-frequency thoughts and

You must let go of your negative thoughts in order to rise up the vibrational scale and away from depression.

feelings out of your mind and your energy vibration will rise, moving you closer to the vibration of love.

Love is the secret

Easier said than done, you might be thinking, and of course you are right; but at least understanding the process is a major step towards achieving it. Once you can look at it in terms of energy, you can see very clearly how the whole process works and this can be very empowering. To perform at your peak, in whatever it is that you are doing, you must attain as high as possible a vibration rate, in terms of your personal energy field. A sports person has to play in the 'zone' to achieve peak performance; a karate expert has to attain a state of 'no mind' to break through piles of building bricks. It's all the same thing: attaining a state of mind with no negativity present. In other words, you have no doubts, you just know you can do it.

We are all falling short

Every single person on this planet has the potential to be 100 per cent of what they can be. Of course, this can mean many different things to many different people. For one person it might be that they have the potential to be the President of the United States of America or the Prime Minister of Great Britain; to another it might be that they have the potential to be an average worker in an average job, or maybe an excellent worker in an above average job. Somebody else may have the potential to be an excellent parent or a very good tennis player. What our potential is doesn't matter, but what does matter is how close we come to achieving it.

The only thing that you can assume for certain here is that 99 per cent of us are not coming anywhere near achieving our potential. In fact, I think it would be a bold statement indeed to say that anybody was truly achieving their potential, as I am sure we are all aware of many improvements that we could make within ourselves. I know for certain that this applies to me, as I always feel that I could do better in whatever it is that I am doing. This, of course, means there is huge room for improvement in just about every area of our lives for every one of us.

We must change how we think

Negative thinking is what holds us back from our potential and when it becomes very severe it can drag us right down into the low zone and result in us suffering some form of depression. To beat depression, the first thing you must do is change your thinking.

Three Steps to a Depression-free Life

This final sections of the book focus on the fundamental issue of raising your average vibrational level so you can help yourself to raise your self-esteem and defeat the depression that is holding you back.

The aim of the exercises is to help you become more high-frequency in your general thinking and eliminate any low-frequency thought patterns that you may have been carrying. This will have the effect of increasing your personal energy frequency, which in turn will push back the barriers of the comfort zone. There are three steps in the process:

‣ **Step 1:** accept responsibility for your life
‣ **Step 2:** make a commitment to creating a depression-free life
‣ **Step 3:** undertake a six-week programme of practical exercises to reprogramme your subconscious mind

I would like you to think carefully about your decision to accept that you are responsible for your life and put this in writing, as this will strengthen your belief. A form of acceptance of your responsibilities is provided (see page 102).

I would like you to dedicate your commitment to this six-week programme to somebody very special to you. A form of dedication is provided for you (see page 106). This will help you to stay focused when your subconscious begins to complain.

Each week you will read out to yourself six high-vibrational affirmations, each one to be read 10 times in the morning and also in the evening. The first affirmation for each week is provided for you, but you must create the other five as part of your task.

You are also required to do a visualisation exercise each day for the six-week period. This is to comfort your inner child and see yourself in a high-vibrational positive situation. A visualisation exercise is provided for you to use in the first week and it is your task to create a new one for each week after that. It is very important to carefully plan your visualisation exercise and write it into your timetable.

The programme for self-improvement that I am setting you is over a six-week period, which in my experience is the optimum time period to initiate change. However, I strongly recommend that you repeat this six-week work model four times with a one-week rest week in between each of the six weeks. This will take you a total of 27 weeks, which is the six months that I personally found cements permanent change.

All this should take you 10 or 15 minutes a day – not much when the results could change your life!

Use the checklists on pages 120–125 to monitor your progress, ticking off the exercises as you do them. This will help you stay focused and bring an element of discipline to your programme.

Accepting Responsibility

Everybody needs to accept full responsibility for their life, as this is the first step to changing for the better and banishing depression for good. Therefore the first step in raising your personal energy vibration on a permanent basis and eradicating depression from your life once and for all is to accept responsibility for depression being in your life.

The act of accepting responsibility for what happens in your life empowers you with control to be able to do something about it. If you don't accept responsibility then you are in effect giving your power away and blaming outside factors for what happens in your life. It is vital to accept the fact that you are in control and can do something about it, to enable you to move forward in a positive and constructive way. You must accept that it is your thoughts that are holding down your energy vibration and not somebody else's. You are in control of your thinking process, so if your mind is filled with negative thought patterns then it is up to you to change that.

The act of acceptance also releases a lot of low-vibrational thought patterns that can flourish in a mind that gives its power away: 'Poor me', 'Why am I so unlucky?', 'Everybody is against me', 'It's not my fault'. These low-vibrational thought patterns serve only one purpose and that is to drag down your energy frequency in the present moment, making life much harder for you in the process. The repercussions of this are that you are much more likely to pull your energy far enough down the vibrational scale to put yourself in danger of suffering from depression. So you can see, step one is vitally important and you cannot move forward until you acknowledge that you are responsible for your life.

Your acceptance statement

I would like you to write down the following acceptance statement and read it out loud to yourself.

> From today, the ..... of ..... 20..., I .... accept full responsibility for my life. I realise that there is no point in holding on to any low-vibrational feelings and emotions from the past. I release any negative energy that I am holding on to. From this moment I accept total responsibility.

Strengthen yourself every day

Repeat this over to yourself, as you see your self letting go of all the low-vibrational energy and allow your energy frequency to rise as you move your life forward into a new and exciting future.

You can read through your acceptance statement any time that you feel your old low-vibrational feelings creeping back in, which may be associated with your previous bouts of depression.

Making the Commitment

You must be totally committed to changing your life for the better if you really want to move forward and eradicate depression from your life once and for all. A very strange thing happens when you truly commit to something; you seem to tap into an extraordinary force. The dramatist Goethe wrote:

> '*The moment one commits oneself then providence moves too. All sorts of things occur to help one that would never have otherwise occurred. A whole new stream of events all manner of unforeseen incidents and chance meetings, and material assistance come forth which no one could have dreamt would appear.*'

Something quite magical occurs when you make a committed decision. When your intention is totally focused you tap into the incredible power of your subconscious mind and enlist its full support in your chosen endeavour. You see, normally your subconscious mind (inner child) sticks to its programme or comfort zone, which places a great deal of restriction on your intentions. You are, in fact, normally held back by your inner child and this becomes the controlling factor in your efforts to achieve your chosen goal. However, when your commitment is total you seem to override the programming and enlist the full support of your inner child (subconscious mind) tapping into your incredible potential in the process.

This total act of surrender by the subconscious only happens on rare occasions when your commitment is so complete that the possibility of failure is not even a consideration. You have in effect disciplined your inner child and it has for once fallen into line, as you are not prepared to settle for anything less.

What real commitment can achieve

I remember a story a policeman told me about one night when he attended a car accident. A young child was trapped under a car and four burly policemen attempted to lift the car off the child. They struggled to no avail; the car was just to heavy to move. Then the mother of the child took hold of the car and lifted it by herself. They looked on in amazement, as this to them had seemed impossible to do. What had in fact happened was that the woman had totally committed herself to lifting the car, and this focused commitment had overridden her programming about what was and wasn't possible. This enabled her to experience no doubts about her strength and consequently she lifted the car with ease.

We are living in a world where we are constantly restricted by beliefs put in place by society, by other people and by our upbringing. The act of commitment overrides these limitations of the mind and enables us to tap into our true potential. This is why after years of trying and many experts saying that it was impossible, once Roger Bannister broke the four-minute mile, within weeks four or five other athletes had also ran the mile in under four minutes. He had simply shown that it could be done.

This is why it is so important to be focused and fully committed to your decision to eradicate depression from your life forever. The more intense your commitment, the fewer problems your subconscious programming will cause you. Just like going on a diet, if you are not totally committed and you half-heartedly watch what you eat your subconscious mind will soon tempt you back off your diet, to where it believes you belong. It can be very resistant to change and will use all of its considerable persuasive powers to keep you within the comfort zone. You must leave no ways out, no maybes or 'we'll see how it goes' attitudes, because this is a sure fire way of guaranteeing failure. You must focus on success; nothing else will do.

Your commitment

The next step is therefore to commit totally to the next six weeks and be focused on your goal. We will work on six weeks because that is a comfortable time period to be able to stay determined and in control without too much interference from your subconscious mind.

I would like you to write the following and read it out loud to yourself:

From today, the ...... of ...... 20 ...., I, ..., commit to focus on my goal with all my strength for the next six weeks. I will succeed in my desire to carry out the exercises and disciplines required, and I will not fail.

Any time that you feel your willpower begin to weaken you can refer back to your dedication to reinforce your commitment.

Dedicate your commitment

A good way to reinforce your commitment is to dedicate your goal to somebody very special to you, perhaps your son or daughter or in memory of a loved one. Do it for them and make them proud of you. It also helps if you can put this dedication in writing, because this confirms your decision and you can refer back to it in moments of weakness.

> *I, ..., dedicate the following six weeks to .... because .... I will make you very proud of me.*

This act of dedication will help sustain you when your inner child (subconscious) starts complaining and your determination and willpower weakens.

Your Affirmations

Affirmations are powerful statements that you repeat to yourself over and over, which eventually your subconscious mind (inner child) accepts as being true. If you continually bombard yourself with these statements, then in effect you are reprogramming your subconscious mind and redefining the boundaries of your comfort zone. Obviously you want to use powerful high-vibrational statements, which you can tailor to your own particular needs. This will have the effect of replacing low-vibrational thought patterns with high-vibrational thought patterns, raising the frequency of your personal energy field in the process. The longer you keep this up, the more permanent the rise in frequency will be.

Affirmations should be written in the present tense as if you have already attained them and I would recommend that you read them to yourself, preferably out loud, every morning and every night just before you go to sleep. Each statement should be read 10 times and you can keep repeating your favourite ones to yourself all day long, whenever you can find the time.

After a couple of weeks you will be amazed at how different you feel; the high-vibrational statements will be raising the frequency of your personal energy field. If after three to four weeks you feel that it's not really working anymore, don't let this deter you, because this is a crucial point when you must keep up the bombardment. Your subconscious mind can be very clever and will use all of its cunning, persuasive powers to resist change, so it's important here that you keep going. I found that my inner child when faced with lack of success went very quiet for a couple of weeks, then when I became a little complacent in my focus it suddenly reappeared and was back up to its old tricks.

After six weeks you will be making progress and the boundaries of your comfort zone will be changing without you realising it. At this point you may want to change some of your statements or even take some time out before you begin your next six-week course of affirmations. Here are some examples that you might use:

▶ I love and approve of myself
▶ My positive energy fills my body with energy and power
▶ I radiate and glow powerful positive energy
▶ I am free from depression

A high-vibrational energy field vibrates faster and expands out much further than a low-vibrational energy field. A very slow-vibrational energy field can close in on you and may create depression.

You could write them on flash cards and keep them in your purse or wallet or stick them on your fridge. In fact, place them anywhere that you will see them as you go about your daily business.

Believe me, you can't bombard your subconscious mind (inner child) enough. You should live and breathe high-vibrational thoughts and they will push up the vibration of your personal energy field, changing your life for the better in the process. It's very simple: the more high-vibrational thoughts that you think, the more used to it your mind will become. In effect, you are drowning out the low-vibrational thoughts and not allowing them to take hold and drag down your personal energy frequency. If you do this enough, your subconscious mind will accept that this is the norm for you and then this will become your natural state of being.

Your Visualisations

Walt Disney said, 'If you can dream it, you can do it.' That's what visualisation is all about.

Visualisation is a very powerful tool that you can use to help reprogramme your subconscious mind. Quite simply, what you are doing with visualisation is convincing your subconscious mind that you are capable of achieving something. The secret to success in any area of your life is just to believe that you can do it, or, to be more precise, to make your subconscious mind believe that you can do it. As the real source of your unlimited potential lies within your subconscious mind, this is where your true capabilities lie.

Belief is the inherent key to success, as to believe truly eliminates any doubts from your mind and moves you into a frequency zone where anything is possible. This is the zone where you are almost bathing in a serene calm and a feeling of happiness brims over inside you. You must detach yourself from the outcome of your objective because to consider the outcome, even for a second, opens the door for doubt to flood in and pull down your frequency, into a less productive zone. The secret is to relax, know that you will succeed and trust in your ability. Just enjoy the moment, basking in the high vibrations, and then almost without thinking of your objective, allow everything to flow naturally and success will be guaranteed.

Learn to see yourself in very positive situations and use this exercise to see yourself happy and joyful. The more you imagine yourself in a positive frame of mind, the more this will become a reality in your life, this will become your comfort zone. Remember: you only have to believe in something to make it a reality.

The key to successful visualisation is your imagination. Learn to use it to your advantage. See yourself in successful situations whether it's at work, in relationships or at leisure. The more you use visualisation, the better you get at it and the easier it is for your subconscious to accept this as real. If you can truly make yourself believe something, then that is the key to making it happen. Visualisation can, of course, be used in just about any area of your life. You may want to use it to help with your job; set aside five minutes each day to visualise how you want your day to

Your expectations are vitally important, as your subconscious mind will manifest into your reality what you expect to get; visualisation can help you to mould your expectations to your advantage.

go, put negative thoughts out of your mind and imagine the best scenario. Maybe you want to use visualisation to improve your relationships; use your imagination to play out any scene that you feel will help and see you and your partner in happy, loving situations.

Practice is the key, and getting yourself into a daily routine will sharpen your imagination and train your subconscious mind to accept your visualisations more readily. This will enable you to control any feelings of depression that may creep over you because practice will have honed your skills, making your subconscious mind open to your suggestions. Visualisation can put you in the driving seat and enable you to control your subconscious mind rather than it being the other way round.

By now you should have accepted that you are responsible for any negativity that may be dragging down your energy field. You should be fully committed to moving your life forward into a new and exciting high-vibrational future, fully focused on eradicating depression from your life once and for all. If you feel comfortable with yourself at this point, we can move on. I will take you through a number of proven and very powerful practical exercises designed to push up the frequency of your personal energy field on a permanent basis, which will help push out the boundaries of your comfort zone.

Comfort your inner child

Comforting your inner child (subconscious mind) is an important exercise and very beneficial in many areas of your life. This will have the effect, firstly, of letting your inner child know that you are acknowledging that they are there, and, secondly, of helping to release any low-vibrational thought patterns that may be rooted within your subconscious mind. These deep-seated low-vibrational thought patterns may have been there for many years,

Comforting your inner child shows it that you love it; when it feels loved it will be much more helpful to you as you negotiate life's hurdles.

causing your personal energy vibration to be held down at the lower frequencies unnecessarily. It is very important when looking to move your life forward that you clear out these low-frequency feelings and emotions. It's extremely difficult to take the positive steps forward when you may be held back in this way. It's like carrying a dead weight and severely hampers your progress if left unattended.

How to visualise

I will take you through a short visualisation exercise. Read through the exercise first, then get yourself comfortable and close your eyes, slowly running through it again in your mind. This exercise can sometimes unearth some very emotional issues from the past. Of course, that is what we are trying to achieve, but if you feel in any way apprehensive, then it may be best to have somebody sit with you for the first few times that you engage in this visualisation. Then they can be on hand to offer support and reassurance if you feel this may be necessary.

The stages of visualisation are:

▸ Read through the visualisation first so you understand what it is trying to achieve and what you need to do
▸ Get yourself comfortable in a warm room, in a comfortable chair or on your bed
▸ Close your eyes and relax
▸ Slowly run through the visualisation in your mind
▸ Once you have completed the visualisation, lie and relax until you are ready to return to the real world again

Comfort your inner child visualisation

The point of this exercise is to see your inner child happy and having fun and most of all to reassure them that you love them. Loving your inner child will help you release any deep-seated low-vibrational thought patterns that may be embedded within your mind, which could push you down into depression.

Imagine yourself sitting on an old stone bench by a beautiful river. You can feel the gentle warm breeze blowing across your face and you gaze out thoughtfully taking in the scene. It's a wonderful day and you look in amazement as a fish jumps up out of the water and plops back into the river. As you sit feeling very relaxed and calm, you hear a noise behind you. You turn and to your surprise see a small child sat on the grass. As you look more carefully you realise that the child is actually you as you were at five years old. This is your inner child and you realise that they look sad and unhappy.

'Don't worry,' you say putting your arms around your child and giving them a gentle hug. 'I love you very much and I will always take care of you.' Pick up your inner child and hold them close, feeling the love between you as you embrace. See a little smile appear on your child's face as they feel warm and protected in your arms. Give them a big hug and say to your child, 'I will never neglect you again, we will have a beautiful happy life and I will never let any harm come to you.'

Your inner child looks at you and you see a big happy smile appear on their face, you give them a gentle tickle and they laugh and giggle with glee. 'Come on,' you say, putting your child on to the ground, and you run after them saying, 'I am going to tickle you!' They laugh uncontrollably and are full of the joys of spring. You end up rolling on the grass in each other's arms, having great fun and very happy.

Keeping in touch with your inner child

Now that you have made contact with your inner child you may find it beneficial to keep up the relationship, and visualisation is a wonderful way of doing this. As you start to use HVT in your life you will become more aware of the constant tussle between your conscious and subconscious mind. When you feel this taking place, it may help if you take a little time to explain to your subconscious mind what it is that you are trying to achieve. Make your inner child part of your life and remember your life will be a lot easier if you can enlist its support in your endeavours.

Explain to it what the benefits to both of you will be if what you are doing works out. Don't forget it is a child, so make it attractive to it. For example, you may be a student taking exams, feeling pretty unsure of your capabilities and in need of all the help you can get. Ask your inner child to help you and explain that if you pass your exams, this will enable you to get a better, higher paid job, which means more treats, such as a new laptop computer or a wide-screen television. Maybe you'll spoil yourself with a large box of chocolates. Remember that you are trying to motivate a five-year-old child, so think in terms of what they would like. Learning to communicate with your inner child is important if you are to move forward and fully realise your amazing potential. After all, it is the thought patterns that are programmed into the mind of your inner child that control and dominate your life and the best way to make changes in this area, is to first of all open the channels of communication.

Your Progress to a Depression-free Life

Use these pages to write your own affirmations, make notes on your personal visualisations and tick off when you have completed tasks. It will help to keep you on track, give you focus and purpose, and also reassure you that things are improving all the time.

My acceptance statement

....
....
....
....

My dedication

....
....
....
....

Week 1
My affirmations

▸ I love and approve of myself.

▸ . . . . ▸

▸ . . . .

▸ . . . .

▸ . . . .

▸ . . . .

My visualisation
Comfort your inner child visualisation (see pages 115–116)

My checklist

Day	Morning affirmations	Visualisation	Evening affirmations
Monday			
Tuesday			
Wednesday			
Thursday			
Friday			
Saturday			
Sunday			

Week 2
My affirmations

▸ I am deserving of love.

▸ . . . .

▸ . . . .

▸ . . . .

▸ . . . .

▸ . . . .

My visualisation
Personalised comfort your inner child visualisation

My checklist

Day	Morning affirmations	Visualisation	Evening affirmations
Monday			
Tuesday			
Wednesday			
Thursday			
Friday			
Saturday			
Sunday			

Week 3
My affirmations

▶ I am very confident and strong.

▶ . . . .

▶ . . . .

▶ . . . .

▶ . . . .

▶ . . . .

My visualisation
Personalised comfort your inner child visualisation

My checklist

Day	Morning affirmations	Visualisation	Evening affirmations
Monday			
Tuesday			
Wednesday			
Thursday			
Friday			
Saturday			
Sunday			

Week 4
My affirmations

▶ I radiate powerful positive energy.

▶ . . . . ▶

▶ . . . .

▶ . . . .

▶ . . . .

▶ . . . .

My visualisation
Personalised comfort your inner child visualisation

My checklist

Day	Morning affirmations	Visualisation	Evening affirmations
Monday			
Tuesday			
Wednesday			
Thursday			
Friday			
Saturday			
Sunday			

Week 5
My affirmations

▶ I have a very powerful presence.

▶ ....

▶ ....

▶ ....

▶ ....

▶ ....

My visualisation
Personalised comfort your inner child visualisation

My checklist

Day	Morning affirmations	Visualisation	Evening affirmations
Monday			
Tuesday			
Wednesday			
Thursday			
Friday			
Saturday			
Sunday			

Week 6
My affirmations

▸ I am totally in control of my life.

▸ . . . .

▸ . . . .

▸ . . . .

▸ . . . .

▸ . . . .

My visualisation
Personalised comfort your inner child visualisation

My checklist

Day	Morning affirmations	Visualisation	Evening affirmations
Monday			
Tuesday			
Wednesday			
Thursday			
Friday			
Saturday			
Sunday			

Index